Social **Media for Trainers**

Techniques for
Enhancing and
Extending Learning

JANE BOZARTH

Pfeiffer

A Wiley Imprint
www.pfeiffer.com

Library of Congress Cataloging-in-Publication Data

Bozarth, Jane.
    Social media for trainers: techniques for enhancing and extending learning / Jane Bozarth.
        p.   cm.
    Summary: "New social media technologies and strategies provide quick, easy solutions to many of the challenges faced by workplace training practitioners. Social media vehicles such as Twitter and Facebook, for example, can help trainers build learning communities, facilitate quick assignments, offer updates or follow-up tips, and otherwise extend the reach of the formal training event. Social Media for Trainers is the first how-to guide on the incorporation of social networking techniques into a trainer's repertoire. It covers the most popular Web 2.0 tools for instructor-created content (blogs), community-created content (wikis), micro-blogging (Twitter), and community sharing and interaction (Facebook), all with detailed instruction on conducting several training/training-related activities."—Provided by publisher.
    Includes bibliographical references and index.
    ISBN 978-0-470-63106-5 (pbk.)
    1. Information society.   2. Social media.   3. Web 2.0.   4. Training.   I. Title.
    HM851.B693 2010
    006.7'54071—dc22

2010017996

Acquiring Editor: Marisa Kelley
Director of Development: Kathleen Dolan Davies
Production Editor: Dawn Kilgore

Editor: Rebecca Taff
Manufacturing Supervisor: Becky Morgan

Printed in the United States of America

Printing   10 9 8 7 6 5 4 3 2 1

About This Book

Why is this topic important?

The advent of Web 2.0 technologies has ignited explosive growth in the use of social media tool and social networking activities. As this book goes to press, two hundred million people check into Facebook daily, and the popular Facebook "Farmville" game is now played by more people than the population of France.

In the workplace we are seeing stunning examples of social networking used to break down silos and build bridges, to grow communities, and to increase the sphere of individuals and work units. Those in need of information need it—and need to know how to find it—in the moment, not when the training department happens to offer it. And they have learned to find that information from one another, rather than depend on traditional, slow, inefficient, and often inaccurate top-down means. It is critical, if workplace trainers intend to remain viable and credible, that they understand how to participate in the networks and use the social media tools to extend their reach and enhance the development of the employees they are charged with developing.

What can the reader achieve with this book?

Trainers making an effort to learn about the tools, experiment with the activities, and engage within social networks will find themselves positioned to enhance the work of the training department and enhance the relationships of trainers and learners, as well as further organizational goals such as retaining talent and sharing tacit knowledge. As discussed in more depth in the book, trainers will be able to implement ways of extending learning into the spaces—in terms of both time and location—between formal training events.

How is this book organized?

This book opens with an overview of social media tools and current trends, as well as a review of key terms. Chapters then provide in-depth coverage of four distinct types of tools: microblogs, communities, blogs, and wikis. Each chapter offers a long list of ideas for activities, discussion topics and formats, and exercises using the tool being discussed. The book concludes with an overview of the bigger picture—social learning—and suggestions for gaining organizational support for change.

Who is this book for?

This book is meant primarily fc   classroom environment. Those engaged in instructional   virtual technologies will find information of use her

About Pfeiffer

Pfeiffer serves the professional development and hands-on resource needs of training and human resource practitioners and gives them products to do their jobs better. We deliver proven ideas and solutions from experts in HR development and HR management, and we offer effective and customizable tools to improve workplace performance. From novice to seasoned professional, Pfeiffer is the source you can trust to make yourself and your organization more successful.

Essential Knowledge Pfeiffer produces insightful, practical, and comprehensive materials on topics that matter the most to training and HR professionals. Our Essential Knowledge resources translate the expertise of seasoned professionals into practical, how-to guidance on critical workplace issues and problems. These resources are supported by case studies, worksheets, and job aids and are frequently supplemented with CD-ROMs, websites, and other means of making the content easier to read, understand, and use.

Essential Tools Pfeiffer's Essential Tools resources save time and expense by offering proven, ready-to-use materials—including exercises, activities, games, instruments, and assessments—for use during a training or team-learning event. These resources are frequently offered in looseleaf or CD-ROM format to facilitate copying and customization of the material.

Pfeiffer also recognizes the remarkable power of new technologies in expanding the reach and effectiveness of training. While e-hype has often created whizbang solutions in search of a problem, we are dedicated to bringing convenience and enhancements to proven training solutions. All our e-tools comply with rigorous functionality standards. The most appropriate technology wrapped around essential content yields the perfect solution for today's on-the-go trainers and human resource professionals.

Pfeiffer
www.pfeiffer.com   *Essential resources for training and HR professionals*

CONTENTS

CHAPTER 1

The Basics   11

CHAPTER 2

Twitter   23

CHAPTER 3
Facebook and Other Communities   53

CHAPTER 4
Blogs   83

CHAPTER 5
Wikis   109

CHAPTER 6
Other Tools   127

CHAPTER 7

The Bigger Picture   143

Afterword: Be the Change   163

LIST OF TABLES AND FIGURES

ACKNOWLEDGMENTS

I am, of course, indebted to the companies discussed in this book, most of which were both quick and gracious about giving permission to use screenshots (and two of which reminded me that I needed to update the versions I was using). Wherever you see "thanks to" or "with permission of" in the text of this book, someone somewhere has reviewed a request and provided a written answer. Special thanks in this regard to Facebook's Leah Pearlman. Also, thanks to Craig Wiggins for his help completing a permissions form in Portuguese.

I am, as ever, appreciative that my employer, the State of North Carolina, and the managers at the Office of State Personnel, have once again been so supportive of my work and so publicly enthusiastic about it.

I am particularly indebted to Jennifer Hofmann, owner of InSync Training, LLC, who over the years has been patient, enthusiastic, supportive, and forgiving, sometimes all at once. I can't thank her enough for providing the untold opportunities that have opened so many doors.

Thanks to Pfeiffer reviewers Dr. Tracey Connolly, Dr. Karl Kapp, and Dr. Clark Quinn, as well as informal reviewers Jeanette Campos and Gloria Melton Mercer, for their helpful, gentle feedback. And thanks as well to my ever-supportive and smart Twitter community. Y'all rock!

As ever, thanks to my husband Kent Underwood, who continues to think it is more cool than annoying to have an author for a wife.

Jane Bozarth
Durham, North Carolina
May 2010

Getting the Most from This Resource

What Will This Book Do for You?

The possibilities for uses of social media to create community and collaboration are dazzling, although the array of tools and their applications can seem daunting. But there is no denying the very popularity of social media. As of this writing, Facebook is the second-most-visited site on the Web (after Google) with more than four hundred million users, more than half of them over the age of twenty-five. On several different days in March 2010, Facebook use spiked ahead even of Google. Two hundred million users visit the site at least once a day. Facebook users upload three *billion* photos a month (data: www.facebook.com). This is not just an American phenomenon: 43 percent of South Koreans maintain a blog (data: www.greenm3 .com/2010/02/most-wired-place-on-earth-south-korea-an-indicator-of-where-we-are-heading.html). It seems nearly everyone who is online has accessed some form of social media, be it a networking site like Facebook, MySpace, or LinkedIn; a private membership community like those available via Ning, or even just browsing YouTube videos or sharing photos via Flickr. New products appear, change, and merge with others every day. New functionality is added as existing tools are upgraded and refined.

The odds are good that you, too, have spent some time on a social media site. Probably you've done this out of a personal interest, on your own time, or perhaps as part of a professional community. Maybe you've just searched for a particular type of training video on YouTube. Even if your experience is minimal, this book will help you better understand the ideas behind social media and also help you understand some of the most popular social media technologies at their root and identify ways of leveraging them to enhance and extend your training programs.

Finally, in a broader sense, learning to leverage social media tools is critical to the future of training departments. Many of us now work in organizations striving toward better collaboration. We may be in organizations with people working globally, perhaps never connecting face-to-face. Workers are insisting on more "teleworking" options. The advent of tools like web-enabled phones make it possible for many people to work quite literally from anywhere. And the coming exodus of the Baby Boomer portion of the workforce demands that we become more adept at sharing knowledge. In short: The trainer who masters social media is positioned to help the organization get where it wants to go.

Who This Book Is for

This book is intended primarily for the workplace training practitioner, working partly or entirely in the traditional four-walled classroom. It will also be of use to those working in delivering training online via web conferencing tools, such as WebEx or Elluminate, and those involved in instructional design work for both traditional and online environments.

The first decade of the 21st century saw rapid growth of web technologies and ideas and tools related to workplace "e-learning" in its many forms. This was sometimes viewed by training practitioners as the provenance of younger generations, referred to in the literature (which has been largely discounted) as "digital natives," who grew up with computer and web technologies. It was common to hear trainers claim that staff were not "tech-savvy" or "preferred face-to-face interaction," even when that was only a gut feeling. Rather, my graduate school research revealed that it was actually more often the Baby Boomer-ish-age trainers themselves—who comprise a large part of the workplace learning industry—who were not tech-savvy and preferred face-to-face interaction. They then appeared to project this onto their beliefs about the younger members of the workforce.

But as technologies have become easier to use, with more personal relevance to the end-users, arguments about learner age or lack of skill at using technology simply don't have any credence. The fastest-growing group on Facebook is made up of those age fifty and older, with those age forty-one to forty-nine right behind; the fastest-growing single demographic among Facebook users is women over age fifty-five. (Data: http://technomarketer.typepad.com/technomarketer/2009/03/the-age-of-facebook-vs-myspace-februarymarch-edition.html). It is evident that, as learner interests and abilities evolve, it behooves those in the workplace training field to keep up. Essentially, developing ways of incorporating social media strategies into training practice is crucial in finding ways to meet learners where they are.

Social Media for Trainers is intended to be useful to those working in the workplace training and learning fields who are brand new to these technologies, as well as those who may be using them at home and wish to transfer their understanding of them into their work roles.

What This Book Covers

This book covers basic considerations about social media in training: what it is, why and how to use it, and how to get started. Tools comprising the main categories of social media technologies (particularly those that support networking) are covered in depth: blogs, wikis, community spaces, and microblogging. Tools that might be considered add-ons to these, such as YouTube, Google Wave, and Skype, are covered in less depth. Specific products were chosen based on their popularity at the time of this writing. Facebook is overwhelmingly the most popular networking site, with four hundred million users as of February 2010; it is, today, the second-most visited website after Google. MySpace offers some functionality and an experience similar to Facebook, but the user base is shrinking; with "only" 124 million unique users visiting during February 2009. (Data: www.guardian.co.uk/technology/2009/mar/29/myspace-facebook-bebo-twitter) It appears MySpace users are aging out of MySpace and moving to Facebook (Data: http://technomarketer.typepad.com). Trainers with a preference (or whose organizations have a preference) for MySpace should be able to generalize much of the Facebook discussion to MySpace application. Similarly, Twitter is by far the most popular microblogging tool, so it was chosen for in-depth discussion here. Information should be generalizable to other microblogging tools.

For each of the technologies there's an explanation of the basics of getting started. This is followed by specific instructions for activities and discussions that can be adapted to many approaches, but often are uniquely suited to the tool being discussed. As technologies are constantly evolving, the activities in the book are offered with an eye toward adaptation to future, as-yet-unknown social media tools.

Disclaimer

This book references a number of websites and particular products. There is always danger when talking about web technologies: Site addresses change, companies merge, and products disappear. Please check my website, www.bozarthzone.com, and my blog http://bozarthzone.blogspot.com for updates, information about changes, or revised links.

Additionally, this book includes a number of screenshots of the social media tools discussed. While interfaces and branding elements remain intact and used per the terms of the products referenced, every precaution has been taken to protect the identity of actual customers. Except where explicitly noted, names have been changed, real photos have been replaced with stock photos, and the text of comments and other materials has been rewritten.

Join In!

Social media is not a spectator sport: The way to learn about social media is to participate. Join me on Facebook (Jane Bozarth Bozarthzone) or on Twitter (@JaneBozarth) to start.

Key Terms

While it's usual to put this sort of thing at the end of a book, it made more sense to list key terms here this time. New technologies have brought with them a whole new world of terms and jargon. I suggest reviewing this list quickly before you move into the discussions of particular products and approaches.

Blog: Short for "web log," a blog provides an online space for posting chronologically ordered comments or ideas that can include text, photo, video, audio, and links to other sites, blogs, or documents. Readers can respond to posted content.

Bookmarking: (also known as "social bookmarking") Web-based bookmarking tools allow users to create and store lists of web resources they wish to share with others. Bookmarks are stored with tags accessible to the public or to those in a selected network, allowing users to search for, say, "animation" or "icebreaker." (See "Tags.") Sites like Del.icio.us and Digg track the popularity of stored bookmarks. Bookmarking is also useful for trainers who travel, as lists of favorite bookmarks can be accessed from any computer with an Internet connection.

CAPTCHA: (Verification Code) Slang for "capture." The letters and numbers you often have to decipher and type in when setting up an account or completing a web-based form. It is a mechanism used to check whether you are a human, not a program auto-completing online forms, and is used to prevent spam or flooding. For instance, many sites that sell concert tickets use a CAPTCHA to ensure that a real person, not a computer, is reserving seats in the online booking system. CAPTCHA is jokingly referred to as "the alphabet soup entrance exam" to enter some sites.

Cloud Computing: In the "old days" data and files were stored on user computers and company servers. In cloud computing, remote servers store and manage data, freeing up memory needs for individual user computers and local servers. Everything is hence stored in a "cloud." Google Docs (for sharing documents), Slideshare. net (for sharing presentation slides), and online file converters are examples of cloud computing likely to be of use to trainers.

Creative Commons Licensing: Creative Commons is a San Francisco-based nonprofit organization. It allows individuals to submit their original work, such as photographs, and provides conditions under which the items can be used. Terms can include requirements, for instance, about attribution, not using for commercial processes, etc. Use of the items licensed is free, but the licensing process allows the person or company to maintain ownership of content while also allowing it to be distributed. See http://search.creativecommons.org for available items.

Google Wave: This is, according to Google, a "personal communication and collaboration tool." It is something like a real-time cross between email, wiki, online chats, and a document generator.

Mashup: A mashup results when content, data, functions, or other material are combined from one or more sources. An example is ZonTube, a mashup that integrates music from Amazon.com with YouTube videos.

MLearning: This is short for "mobile learning." Some interpret this to mean learning via some sort of device, such as a smartphone (see "smartphone" below) or even cell phone with texting capability. Specific products and software applications for mobile devices are mentioned later in this book; many activities described are quite appropriate for participation via a device. Others define Mlearning as inclusive of anything a learner can do via any means in a "mobile" way, including, for instance, printing out a copy of a PDF and reading it on the train during the daily commute to work.

Read-Write Web: This is a reference to the advent of tools allowing for easy user-generated content, such as wikis and blogs.

RSS ("really simple syndication"): Rather than go out and look at your favorite blogs and news sites each day, you can subscribe to them and have any updates delivered directly to you. You need to set up a free RSS reader, available from many sites, including Yahoo, Google, Netvibes, Bloglines, PageFlakes, and Newsgator. Once you have chosen a reader, which will usually reside on a personal page like your iGoogle page or your Yahoo home page, you can begin subscribing to RSS feeds. Look on your favorite blogs and news sites for the orange RSS icon (shown in figure I.1) to subscribe to an RSS feed.

You will be given either a dropdown of icons of popular readers, like the ones shown, or you'll be presented with a page of code. If you see an icon that matches your favorite reader, as shown in Figure I.2, just click on it and you will receive the feed.

Figure I.1. RSS Feed Icon

Figure I.2. RSS Reader Buttons

If you see a page of code rather than a button for your reader, then copy and paste the page URL from the top of the screen into your own reader via the "add a subscription" link. Updates to blogs and news sites will be delivered to your reader.

SharePoint: This is a Microsoft product or, more precisely, a collection of for-purchase products, designed to work together within the enterprise. Products are grouped into the categories Collaboration, Processes, and People. Depending on which items an organization chooses to purchase and install, users have access to shared workspaces, collaborative websites, documents, wikis, blogs, and other tools.

Smartphone: Web-enabled cell phones such as BlackBerry, iPhone, and Droid.

Social Bookmarking: See "Bookmarking."

Social Media: This term refers to online material produced by the public. This is distinct from content produced by professional writers, journalists, or generated by the industrial or mass media. Examples of social technologies used to create social media include those for communication (such as blogs), collaboration (such as wikis), communities (such as Facebook), reviews and opinions (such as Amazon reader reviews), and multimedia (such as YouTube). The term "social media" is sometimes used to refer to the tools themselves.

Streisand Effect: Online phenomenon in which an attempt to censor or block information has the unintended result of drawing additional attention to it. The name comes from when actress Barbra Streisand sued a photographer for publishing pictures of the California coastline, including photos of her home, on a website. The resulting publicity drew nearly half a million viewers to the site.

Tags/Tagging: Tags are keywords assigned to content to facilitate its retrieval. They are a classification tool used by the creator or the user. The classification is informal. For instance, when using the Flickr photo sharing service/website, I might tag a photo of my dog as "dog" "Welsh corgi," and "Donald."

Web 2.0: Refers to the advent of many technologies that allow users to easily—and often for free—create, publish, and share their own content via the Internet. This is in contrast to "Web 1.0," the time during which those with programming expertise created mostly static web pages. Blogs, wikis, and YouTube are examples of Web 2.0 tools.

Widget: A piece of programming code that can be inserted into any web page, such as an event countdown or stock market ticker. A *gadget* is a widget, but it is proprietary. For instance, Google offers gadgets like "virtual sticky notes" and weather updates that only work with other Google products, such as a Blogger blog or iGoogle home page.

Wiki: An interactive web page on which everyone with access can change the content. Changes can be tracked and time-stamped so they can be reviewed later if desired. "Wiki" is Hawaiian for "quick," and that is where the tool's name originated, but in recent years "wiki" has been retroactively described as an acronym for "What I Know Is."

Ready? Let's begin by reviewing some basics of using social media for workplace learning.

CHAPTER 1

The Basics

What Is Social Media?

As I said in the "Key Terms" section of the Introduction, the term "social media" refers to online material produced by the public, distinct from content produced by professional writers, journalists, or generated by the industrial or mass media. Examples of social technologies used to create social media include those for communication (such as blogs), collaboration (such as wikis), communities (such as Facebook), reviews and opinions (such as Amazon reader reviews), and multimedia (such as YouTube).

The idea of social media is an outgrowth of the concept of "Web 2.0." This is distinct from the early days of online material, which has come to be known as "Web 1.0." Where Web 1.0 offered static web pages created by a few individuals, Web 2.0 technologies invite everyone to create and share content. Table 1.1 offers a comparison of Web 1.0 and Web 2.0.

Think back to your own experience using the Internet. Ten years ago, a person who wanted to create a simple web page with pictures, links, and video had to have some knowledge of programming and skill at working with graphics and multimedia, needed FTP software for uploading the files, and required access to a server to put them on.

Five years ago, a person who wanted to create a simple web page with pictures could create a blog and, upon logging in, had tools for adding things like pictures and links. That person then had to find ways to draw readers to the blog. Someone wanting to just share pictures needed a login and account for that (Flickr, Snapfish), then needed to notify

Table 1.1. Comparison of Web 1.0 to Web 2.0

Web 1.0	Web 2.0
Programmer-created web pages, graphics, Flash	User-created Web pages, pictures, user reviews, blogs, wikis, YouTube, social networks
Experts create content	Everyone creates content
Individuals visit web pages, read content	People construct shared information
Tightly controlled "sites"	Loosely controlled communities
One-way (one-to-many)	Many-to-many (and peer-to-peer)
Britannica Online	Wikipedia
Publish	Participate
Firewalls, hierarchies	Dynamic, non-hierarchical
Static, stable content, few changes	Constantly updated content (Twitter, Wikipedia)

others that pictures were there; someone wanting to share video needed a YouTube account and login. Typically, each tool employed had its own site, separate login, and often a separate learning curve for the user.

Nowadays (assuming you have at least seen Facebook), consider what is available to even the minimally skilled computer user: a one-login place that aggregates all the features of the other sites. You set up one account, log in once, and can post thoughts, participate in discussions, and share pictures, videos, and links. It is truly different, much more democratic, and decidedly more empowering than the "old days" of Web 1.0.

So, if nothing else, try to look at the tools for their ability to empower individuals. They allow for ease in creating and sharing content, support conversation and collaboration, help to connect people in disparate roles, and reduce barriers of time and geography. The Afterword in this book offers my thoughts on the bigger implications of effective use of social media in organization-wide initiatives, such as managing knowledge, preserving institutional memory, creating transparency, and enhancing communication. For now, let's examine how social media can be of particular use to training practitioners as they enact their work.

Why Social Media in Training?

The effective use of social media strategies to supplement, or use in place of, traditional training endeavors can provide a big payoff for both learners and trainers. For one, the technologies dissolve many of the barriers between the learners and the instructor, creating a more informal, collegial, and interactive learning environment.

Trainers and learners frustrated with elements of the traditional approach will find some relief through using social media. It can provide a vehicle for continuing conversations beyond the time constraints of the workshop schedule. It can extend the learning process beyond the confines of the classroom space and support development of communities of learners. It's important to realize that, even if (as a trainer) you do not find traditional instruction frustrating, many of your learners—as noted in the Introduction—have made their interest in and acceptance of online interaction clear. Again, social media tools can help the trainer meet learners where they are.

Training strategies incorporating social media tools can help learners become more aware of their own learning process, more mindful of and deliberate about their own learning, and encourage them to take ownership of learning and then apply it to their jobs. Perhaps most importantly, effective use of social media in training can provide additional support for sustaining new learning and transferring formal training back to the workplace; this is essentially the focus of the book, and you will see many examples as you go through the individual chapters. And finally, thoughtful use of social media in training can provide additional support for, and room to include, the training department in the informal learning so critical to job success.

The traditional model of workplace training and development tends to look much like Figure 1.1. In the span of a twenty-year career with a company, this supervisor attended a two-day new hire orientation

Figure 1.1. Typical Formal Training Events Throughout a Career

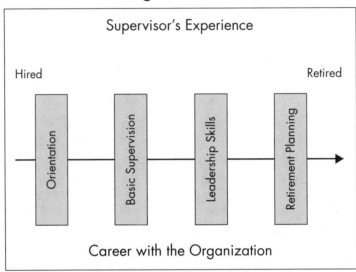

Used with permission of Bob Mosher.

program, a six-module supervisory skills course, a leadership development program, and finally a retirement planning seminar. Along the way there likely were other training events, such as compliance updates, training in new processes or procedures, and workshops on using new software or equipment. But the vast bulk of this worker's time was spent on the job, not in a structured training event.

Consider our supervisor in the example shown in Figure 1.2 instead. She is spending many, many more hours engaged in informal learning activities (although she may not always recognize these as "learning"): coaching from the next-level manager, meetings with a chosen or assigned mentor, and casual conversations in the hallway or at the water cooler. She is learning via the "Hey, Joe!" phenomenon: "Hey, Joe! How do I reformat these tables again?" "Hey, Joe! What did you say was the trick to getting these contracts through so quickly?" She is reading, viewing online tutorials, and, yes, learning by trial and error. Research (Dobbs, 2000; Kupritz, 2002) indicates that as much as 70 percent of workplace learning is informal, occurring outside the classroom and in

Figure 1.2. Most Learning Occurs in the Spaces Between Formal Training Events

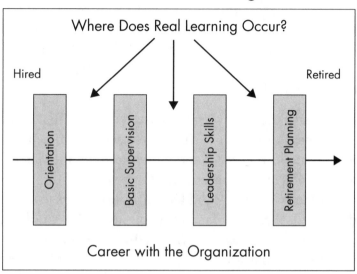

Where Does Real Learning Occur?

Hired

Retired

Orientation

Basic Supervision

Leadership Skills

Retirement Planning

Career with the Organization

Used with permission of Bob Mosher.

the spaces between formal training events. Social media is one way for the training department and the training practitioners to get into those spaces and reach employees between events. In essence, training approaches incorporating social media strategies more closely resembles how we really learn in our day-to-day activities.

Which One?

At present there are literally dozens of social media tools available. Experience has shown that, over time, products tend to consolidate as a few clear "winners" emerge. The tools I have chosen to cover in-depth in this book are the ones most popular at the time of this writing and the ones that seem most likely to be around for a few years. But they were also chosen for their distinct differences: microblogging (Twitter), blogging, community (Facebook), and collaborative editing (wikis). Other products replicate or combine these functions. Whatever you choose to use—and whatever future products bring—it is critical that you experiment and learn to see technologies for what they really are.

Blogging tools, for instance, really provide very easy means of creating clean, simple, professional-looking web pages. We'll be going through the tools one at a time, from Twitter to Facebook, then to blogs and wikis, and then look at some add-ons like YouTube and SlideShare. Understanding the technologies at their roots will help you make good choices and adapt ideas in this book to whatever new tools you may encounter in the future.

In choosing the technologies to use, remember that every additional site to check, every different user ID and password to remember, every new interface to learn, creates another obstacle for the learner. Try to meet your learners where they are and take them where your organization wants to go For instance, Facebook and LinkedIn allow users to create group pages with discussions. Because so many people are on Facebook and tend to check in often, it's the product discussed in this book. But, depending on your learners, you may want to explore adapting the ideas here for the similar structure of LinkedIn. Consultants and sales reps may have the need to accumulate many business contacts and identify future prospects. They may all have LinkedIn accounts and may choose to log in there every day to make new contacts and check in with groups. In that case, you might choose to utilize LinkedIn with your workforce. Your organization may be using the at-cost MS SharePoint product; it contains many of the same blog and wiki features that the "outside the firewall" applications discussed in this book share. Try to identify the tools your organization's employees are already using or those that are likely to meet their real needs.

According to Deloitte data, 47 percent of Baby Boomers maintain a profile on a social site. Of those, 73 percent are Facebook users, while 13 percent use LinkedIn.

Deloitte, *State of the Media Democracy* (4th ed.), 2009.

Choosing What to Use When

Think of the different technologies as "tools," for that's what they really are, and choose the one that suits your instructional goals. Facebook is a hammer, a wikis is a saw, and each is suited to different overarching goals. It is tempting—and I am often asked—to offer one answer for a given situation. (As in, "If you want to have a community, then use Facebook. If you want to do collaborative work, use a wiki.") It just isn't that simple. Many different tools can support a community: It may surprise you to hear that my own "best" community, for my own development, exists among my Twitter contacts. Most tools will allow you to have discussions or do collaborative work. You'll need to choose things that support your instructional goals, but also those that your organization will allow (perhaps Facebook instead of MySpace, or an inside-firewall microblogging tool instead of Twitter), what your organization already has in place (perhaps a company Facebook page or blog) and what your users are already using and/or will accept. You also need to choose tools that you are comfortable using and will work to support: as you'll see in Chapter 4, a blog may not be the best choice for the trainer who doesn't like to write.

It's tempting, too, to become "tool happy": "I'll use a blog, but we'll add on some Twitter activities, and link back to a wiki." Think through what you are trying to accomplish, identify tools that will help you get there, and stick with your instructional plan. Also try not to change horses mid-stream: If the blog isn't working as you'd hoped, don't ask learners to suddenly switch to a wiki. Talk with them about how to make the blog work for the group. Be flexible, but also be mindful of demands on your learners—you want to support learning, not create confusion.

In this book I try to help you choose the tool or tools you need. They are all the means to an end (better transfer of learning, more engagement in the learning process, growth of a learning community, support for informal learning), but they are not ends in themselves. The point is not to "do" Twitter any more than it is to "do" e-learning. Always consider: "What do my learners need? How can I help them find it?" And stay alert—as tools change, evolve, and come and go—to new possibilities.

The issue is not the technological widget but the means by which interaction around the technology is enabled.

Phillip D. Long, Centre for Educational Innovation and Technology–Brisbane; comment on Twitter October 20, 2009, as @RadHertz.

Getting Started

It's Mostly About Facilitation, and You Already Know How to Do That

Before you begin, particularly if you find this all somewhat daunting, consider this: You are already, more or less, doing this. As a trainer, you already possess skills critical to facilitating and guiding discussion, drawing out quieter participants and managing louder ones, and recapping conversations. You know how to facilitate a role play or respond to a challenging participant. You have a repertoire to bring to bear on activities, even if you are guiding them in a new environment. You will find that your past experience serves you well in supporting and facilitating interactions with social media tools.

Extending the Training Experience

It is important in using social media that you move learners toward working together, toward building community, not just posting an answer in response to you. Encourage dialogue, debate, and interaction. It is possible to be collegial and personal without revealing private details. For instance, asking people to post a photo of a pet, a link to the website of their alma mater, or a golf course they'd like to play helps to build connections and identify similar interests without invading privacy.

Providing Practice Opportunities

Most of the social media technologies described in this book are easy to use in a discuss-this, answer-that format. That's fine, if the questions invite real reflection, thought, reasoning behind ideas, and application of judgment in using critical skills. But learners on a shop floor need to actually use the forklift. Other workers need to use their computers. They need to analyze the data. Or they need to manage people, make cold sales calls, or build a team. Be sure that your approaches include real opportunities for practice. As described in the individual chapters, "practice" can take many forms.

Supporting the Learners

Nothing else you do—lesson planning, careful design, thoughtful choice of technologies—will matter if your learners struggle through the training. Take steps to make the experience painless and positive for them:

- Make the social media site(s) easy to find. Put your Twitter handle, blog URL, or Facebook name on handouts, your organization's website, and in your email signature.

- Provide ample instruction in setting up accounts and using the tools. The products described in this book all offer easy setup guides, and most offer good tutorials. YouTube is also a good resource for information on using different products. Remember that some learners will just need a "quick start" overview; others will need more in-depth help.

- Encourage collaboration; do not force friendships. You can, for example, set up a Facebook group or fan page and invite your learners to join you there. They do not have to become your Facebook "friends" or set up "friend" relationships with other class members. They can access the group or site and participate without everyone else being privy to what is on their own personal pages.

- On the one hand, provide clear guidelines and deadlines. For instance, if you are asking learners to read and respond to one another's blog posts, then the authors will need to have their posts up by a certain date so the others have time to read them. If learners are engaging in a collaborative project, then ask them to be sure to check in regularly (and define "regularly." Do you mean once a day or twice a week?).

- On the other hand, don't micromanage. While providing clear guidelines and deadlines is necessary, organizations and their trainers seem overly concerned with learners who may post inappropriate or critical comments. Some instructors feel the need to over-control and direct conversation toward some desired end, and this sometimes can appear manipulative. Worse, too many rules can discourage participation. Take a look at Figure 1.3, an organization's guidelines for participating in the employee discussion forum. Can you see why hardly anyone does?

Figure 1.3. Too Many Rules Discourage Participation

Rules for Posting	
Do's	Don'ts
Keep it respectful.	Don't use any speech that is inaccurate, unlawful, harmful, defamatory, vulgar, obscene, profane, hateful, racially or ethnically objectionable, personal attacks, antagonistic, threatening, abusive, or harassing to other users or the general public.
Share information that is helpful and public.	Don't post proprietary information, trade secrets, or confidential information.
Keep it relevant.	Don't post advertisements, solicitations, chain letters pyramid schemes, investment opportunities, or other unsolicited commercial communication.
Use it wisely.	Don't spam.
Use a descriptive title for your post.	Don't insinuate or suggest that any statements made by you are endorsed by us.
Read other responses before you post.	Don't post personal ads.
Further the discussion.	Don't use UPPERCASE. This is the same as shouting.
Relate personal expriences.	Don't give out personal information.
Ask for clarification.	Don't use vague subjects lines like "?", etc.
Put yourself in the customer's shoes.	Don't repeat information already provided.
Get to the point.	Don't excessively quote previous messages.
Be positive.	Don't get off topic.
Be understanding.	Don't make assumptions.
Know when to back off.	Don't dole out truisms. (You get what you pay for.)
Focus on your area of expertise.	Don't overwhelm with inofmation.
Make correct spelling and grammar a priority.	Don't trash products, ideas, or people.

Finally: Walk the Talk

In order to be effective at using social media, you have to start participating in social networking activities and develop fluency with the tools. If nothing else, set up Facebook, Twitter, and LinkedIn accounts. Use them as you follow along with this book. Find some blogs to read (search "google blog finder" for topics like training, e-learning, or adult learning). You won't learn about Twitter by having someone "explain" Twitter. You need to join and participate in order to learn how to use it as an effective training tool. Likewise, take a stab at trying out the many features available in Facebook. Find and link to a video clip. Upload some photos. Start a work-related discussion among like-minded colleagues. Work toward the goal of becoming, in the early 21st century, the "Networked Trainer" (Figure 1.4).

Figure 1.4. The Networked Trainer

Image adapted from original with permission of Alec Couros and Silvia Rosenthal Tolisano.

Summary

The trainer using social media thoughtfully will find it a wonderful new means of engaging learners, extending the learning experience, and supporting transfer of new learning to the workplace. Effective strategies can additionally extend the reach of the trainer and the training function, positioning training not just as an event, but as part of the learners' daily lives. In reading through the chapters addressing different technologies and activities, keep on simmer in the back of your mind the topics you teach, the strategies you already use, and the way activities would fit into your particular content and style.

Twitter

In a Nutshell

Twitter is a microblogging tool that allows users to publish chronologically ordered "tweets" of 140 characters or less.

In a Larger Container

Twitter allows you to publish chronologically ordered "tweets" of 140 characters or less. These feed into a public timeline that you and others can view. Think of this timeline as a stream you can limit, choosing people to follow; only their tweets will show up when you log in. Others can then follow you, and your tweets will show up in their streams.

How to View Twitter

Those who read tweets are meant to drink from the stream. You'll see in this chapter that, while as a trainer you can manage discussion and assignments to some extent, Twitter is not in general a vehicle for linear, structured conversation.

Advantages/Disadvantages of Twitter in Training

Advantages

Twitter is a wonderful tool for sharing quick ideas, links, and articles. It offers the user access to industry experts, authors, like-minded practitioners, fellow hobbyists, and, yes, celebrities. It is a pure communication tool, with a quick flow of information and a single feed available to all users (unless you choose to block a particular user or one chooses to block you). It's a great place to find help or advice: Some describe it as a "virtual water cooler." The 140-character limit teaches one to be concise and get to the point.

Twitter users find they can extend their reach far beyond their circle of friends or the walls of their employing organization. Twitter is very interactive, with something going on all the time. Additionally, users do not have to log in to receive updates, but can receive tweets via an RSS feed delivered with other feeds to an RSS reader or to some email clients (Outlook is one).

Disadvantages

Twitter can be frustrating for linear, sequential thinkers and trainers who need a great deal of control. It is "messy," which makes it uncomfortable for some. While there are tools that will allow for management, such as archiving and searching, that really isn't the point. Twitter is mainly meant to be a real-time stream from which users can drink.

Also, some find Twitter's 140-character limit frustrating, constraining their ability to convey subtlety. On a personal note: Most instruction is designed in a sequential, linear fashion to accommodate those who think that way and delivered at a speed to accommodate the most deliberate thinkers in a session. I am not a linear, sequential thinker. I think quickly and find Twitter conversations both energizing and engaging. I also think it's nice to see something used that suits MY needs and preferences for a change!

In considering who to follow and deciding what you want in your stream, keeping an open mind can help you find interesting people who have new or interesting things to say. I mostly follow people in the training, learning, and instructional technology fields, but we aren't all-work-and-no-play. While we talk primarily about work and our projects and interests, we do sometimes share some personal information; this helps us to connect and develop relationships and to sometimes find additional areas of interest. People who have never tried Twitter have sometimes heard popular lore about it being a place where people just tweet about what they had for breakfast. Some do, and if that's all they have to say, then I don't follow them. But sometimes even posting about breakfast can be more than it appears, as when my Twitter friend @lonniehodge posts comments about breakfast where he works—in China; when @paul_steele tweeted about what he had for breakfast—as he was climbing Mount Aconcagua, the highest mountain in the Americas, to raise funds for leukemia research; or when @lancearmstrong posts what he had for breakfast before a race.

Why Twitter Instead of Something Else?

The informal, quick nature of Twitter sets it apart from other Web 2.0 tools. Whereas people might spend a long time composing a comment to a blog post or engage in lengthy, in-depth conversation on a discussion board, Twitter invites more in-the-moment interactions. It provides an easy way to maintain connections, share thoughts, or ask for advice.

Twitter has also been described as "email 2.0." It's quick and to the point, and those who want to see it can access it when they like. The 140-character limit keeps people from turning messages into lectures. It requires only an Internet connection (even on a phone) without having to log in to company email from the road, and links won't be blocked, as they are by some company email setups. You and your learners don't have to keep up with email addresses. Since conversations are public, people can see them, follow them, click on links to articles or videos or photos they include, forward them on to others, and jump in if they have something to add.

Email is where knowledge goes to die.

Bill French: http://bfrench.info/

Why Twitter in Addition to Something Else?

As you'll see in this chapter, Twitter is an excellent place for building and sustaining community, offering quick updates or comments, inviting in-the-moment reflections, and supporting informal discussion.

It's thus good for supplementing traditional classroom-based instruction, asynchronous e-learning programs, virtual classroom instruction, and other training methods for delivering training, and is excellent for supporting the on-boarding of new learners. It is one of the best tools for "filling in the spaces" between formal learning events.

Getting Started

Set Up an Account—or Several Accounts

An account can relate to any entity you choose. For instance, you can set up an account for yourself, for your current session of a course, for a particular topic, or for all learners who engage in any training you offer. Simply go to www.twitter.com to begin the free account creation process.

Choose Your Twitter Handle

Your handle is your Twitter user name or other name your account will have. Be aware that your handle is part of the 140-character count, so choose something short. Instructor Susan Reddington might go with just SusanRed; if creating an account for her leadership course she might go with AcmeLead11 or Lead2011; if creating an account for all graduates of her leadership course, she might choose something like AcmeGrads.

Create Your Profile

Twitter will ask you to provide a short description of yourself and your interests. If you are using Twitter to support a course, you may just say something like: "Acme Leadership course, spring 2001." If you are using Twitter to engage with a broader audience, consider that most followers will look at your profile before deciding to follow you. Make your profile interesting to the folks who interest you. The profile section also asks for a link to your organization, your course site, or your blog, so that people can easily be directed to more information about you and your work.

Get Going

You've no doubt heard of celebrity Twitterers like Oprah Winfrey, Ashton Kutcher, and Alyssa Milano. Type their names into the search area on the Twitter screen; click the button that says "follow" to see their tweets appear on your page. Try looking for others in the training or learning fields who might have ideas of interest to you. Prolific learning and e-learning Tweeters include Stephen Downes, Jay Cross, Marcia Conner, Mark Oehlert, Clark Quinn, Cammy Bean, Dave Ferguson, and Jane Bozarth. Look at who we follow and respond to. When you see a comment you'd like to respond to or a conversation that interests you, just jump in. You don't need to wait to be invited; the fact that people choose to tweet for the world to see *is* your invitation to respond. Once you start tweeting you'll soon see that people start following you. While it is easy to sit back and watch the stream go by, it's critical that you engage with others if you want to have a positive experience with Twitter.

Finding Topics and People

The Twitter search box searches for words and word strings that have recently appeared in tweets. Try searching for e-learning, training, trainers, and instructional design. A Twitter's user handle will also come up via the search box, since that appears in the feed: JaneBozarth (one word), Quinnovator (Clark Quinn), or AplusK (Ashton Kutcher). If you're looking for someone but don't know the person's Twitter handle, you can search for him or her via the "Find People" link at the top of the screen. There, type in Ashton Kutcher, Clark Quinn, or Jane Bozarth to find our Twitter handles.

To post a tweet to anyone following you—and to the public timeline— just type it in:

New article on social learning at www.article.com

Does your organization provide tuition assistance?

How do I edit clip art in PowerPoint?

To reply to someone, use the @ symbol:

@janebozarth Just read that and agree the author makes a lot of assumptions

@janebozarth Can you say more about training having no ROI?

To cite another Twitter user:

Reading @janebozarth's article on social learning at www.article.com

To contact the Twitter user directly, send a direct private message or DM:

Type d, space, then type the username, or use the "direct message" link on your Twitter page. For example: d @janebozarth Why do you say there's no ROI in training? Contradicts what I've heard

In using DMs remember: "Privacy" in regards to Web technologies is a nebulous term.

Deeply personal comments or feedback might best be delivered via another vehicle. *Note:* Following someone automatically means *you allow them* to DM you. Those *you follow* may not allow that. Some Twitterers, particularly celebrities, disable their followers' ability to DM them. Click on the user profile; you can see whether they will accept DMs.

To repeat something you have seen on Twitter:

"Retweet" it with the letters RT, then space, before the @username

For instance: RT @janebozarth there's no such thing as ROI of training

Use a hashtag # to organize conversation around a keyword, topic, or event:

A "hashtag" is the # symbol followed by a word (#election, #oprah) or acronym denoting an event (#ASTD2012, denoting the ASTD 2012 conference). Adding this to each tweet makes the conversation easier to follow. Users type #ASTD2012 into the Twitter search box, and all tweets using that hashtag will appear in the search results.

In this way the results will show users only tweets related to the ASTD 2012 conference, not everything related to the ASTD national organization or local chapters.

Hashtags are created by individual users starting a conversation or by event organizers who let followers know what hashtag that will be used during the event.

@janebozarth book's main idea is that good e-learning is about design, not software #betterthanbulletpoints.

Conferences now publicize the hashtags users should employ in tweeting from the conference site or sessions. Organizers for the Training 2010 conference in San Diego asked attendees to use the hasthag #training2010 in tweeting conference talk:

SusanRed In @janebozarth's session on google apps #training2010

Bill_Gray Headed to Starbucks on concourse A - tweet if you want to meet up there #training2010

Figure 2.1 Shows a typical Twitter screen using the protocols described above.

Figure 2.1. Use of the @, RT, and # Symbols in a Twitter Stream

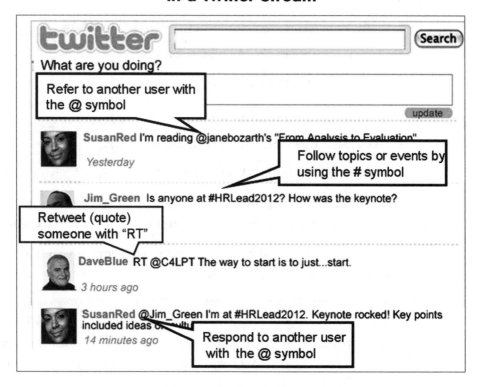

As you'll see throughout this chapter, you may choose to:

- Have your learners follow you, in which case you can ask them to participate by using a hashtag of your choosing.

- Or you may set up an account for the group enrolled in this particular offering of the course.

- Or you may set up an account for all learners who ever took the course.

Going Mobile

You can send and receive tweets via your mobile phone by texting messages:

- Via your country's short code:
  - U.S.: **40404**
  - Canada: **21212**
  - UK: **86444** (Vodafone, Orange, 3 and O2 customers)
  - India: **53000** (Bharti Airtel customers)
  - Indonesia: **89887** (AXIS and 3 customers)
  - Ireland: **51210** (O2 customers)
  - Australia: **0198089488** (Telstra customers)
  - New Zealand: **8987** (Vodafone and Telecom NZ customers)

Be aware that, while Twitter does not charge for this, your mobile phone carrier's texting rates will apply per the terms of your service contract.

- Via Twitter's mobile website http://m.twitter.com if you have a web browser on your mobile phone.

- Via free applications for BlackBerry, iPhone, and other smartphones. Figure 2.2 shows the view of the feed for the "management now" account from the free iPhone application Tweetie2 (soon to change to "Twitter for iPhone"). Class members are discussing project management and are using the hashtag #pm

Figure 2.2. Tweetie2 Is a Free iPhone Application

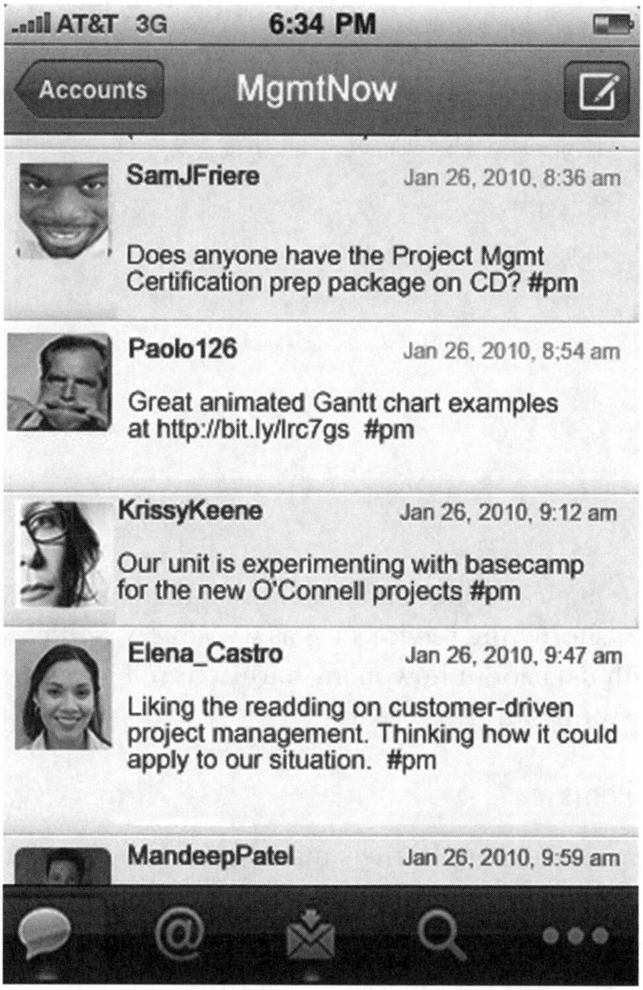

Tweeting by Email

As shown in Figure 2.3, your Twitter account settings will let you choose to receive a number of items via email, including notification of new followers and copies of any direct messages sent. At the top of the Twitter screen choose Home > Settings.

URL Shorteners

Since you are limited to only 140 characters, you'll find that sending links to articles or websites can be challenging. Twitter will

Figure 2.3. Twitter Settings Allow You to Receive Information via Email

automatically shorten long URLs, but you may also choose to use a free shortening service such as www.bit.ly (which will provide you with data about how many have accessed a link you suggest) or www.tinyurl.com.

Sentence Stems

One way to help learners manage the 140-character limit is to provide them with sentence stems—they need only to complete the thought. For example: "One thing that concerns me about the new shipping protocol is. . . ."

GroupTweet

If you want to manage your class as a private unit, a free tool from www .grouptweet.com will convert a standard Twitter account into a group space where members can send tweets to everyone in the group using direct messages. When this group account receives a direct message from a group member, GroupTweet converts it into a tweet that all followers can see. New Twitter tools appear all the time, so search the web for other similar products.

Scheduled Twitter Chats

A number of groups gather regularly on Twitter to discuss topics of interest. These are usually organized by one or more moderators, who publicize the events and perhaps capture a transcript of the conversation. Search for the event by hashtag to see information and recent tweets. Popular events for learning professionals include #lrnchat (Thursdays, 8:30 p.m. ET) and #KMers (discussions of knowledge management, Tuesdays at noon ET). Twitter chats evolve and change, and new chats pop up all the time. Try Googling "Twitter chat" and see what comes up.

Before the Training Event

Prior to the first class gathering, use Twitter to do quick introductions and pre-course assessments.

Introductions

Ask learners to introduce themselves. Say:

- Please tell us your name, location, and job title.

- Please tell us your name, location, and one thing you would like to learn in this training.

- Please tell us your name and the "three keywords" that represent your mission, philosophy, focus, or priorities.

- Please tell us your name and single biggest challenge you face in performing at your best.

You can adapt traditional icebreaker topics for use in Twitter: "Share something personal about yourself: your favorite book or movie, your idea of a dream vacation, your best day ever at work, etc.," or make your request for introductory information more training-topic specific:

- What is your biggest challenge in delivering effective customer service?

- Please tell us your name, location, and the biggest challenge you face as a new supervisor.

- What is one thing you already know about this topic?

- What is one thing you want to know about this topic?

- What training have you already had on this topic?

- What did you find most difficult during your first week on the job?

- Please share the best leadership advice you ever received.

- Please share the most helpful feedback you ever received.

- Please share your one best tip for a new hire.

- Please share the most unhelpful performance review feedback you ever received or heard of another receiving.

You may choose to further engage with the learners, to begin conversation prior to class. Figure 2.4 shows an example (remember to read from bottom to top).

Figure 2.4. Conversation in Twitter

Pre-Work

Twitter is an excellent vehicle for meeting your learners and getting a feel for their training needs, interests, and expectations.

Say:

- Prior to class, please read the article "Safety Strategies for the 21st Century" at www.acme.com and be prepared to discuss it.

- Please review the list of safety issues at www.acme.com and choose the one or two most relevant to your own situation.

- Please prepare your personal mission statement and bring it to class

- Please see the video at www.youtube.com/bozarth3. Prepare a list of three questions you would ask in this situation.

- For the next three days please try to keep a detailed list of your activities: meetings, hallway conversations, time spent on email, etc.

- Prior to class, please Google "emotional intelligence." What are the benefits of developing in this way?

Figure 2.5 shows an example of pre-work in Twitter.

Figure 2.5. Pre-Work in Twitter

twitter   Home Profile Find People Settings Help Sign out

Please review the list of safety issues at http://www.acme.com and choose the one or 2 most relevant to your situation. #acmesafe

11 minutes ago from UberTwitter   Reply Retweet

Jason Willensky
jwillensky

Photo courtesy Jason Willensky @jwillensky.

In Class

The stream created as people tweet during classes or live conference sessions is known as the "backchannel." (If you've spent much time in webinar-type classes, you've seen the running participant text chat that often occurs during sessions. The Twitter backchannel can look much like that.) For some reason this one seems to be hard for trainers, who take it as a sign of disrespect or inattention. But why is someone typing on a BlackBerry different than their writing notes on a legal pad? They can send tweets as a recap of the session to themselves, to co-workers not in attendance, or even to their bosses, who—most trainers wish—were more aware of what happens in training.

This can also provide the trainer with insight as to what people are finding useful, what they question, and, yes, where they are becoming inattentive. *Learning in 3D* co-author Karl Kapp encourages use of a Twitter backchannel during his conference presentations and in his work as a college professor by students enrolled in his courses: "It's good to look at and review the tweets on break to get a sense of the students' state of mind." See the "Formative Evaluation" section later in this chapter on using Twitter for formative evaluation.

Here are tweets sent by Cammy Bean during a session I was presenting about my book *Better Than Bullet Points: Creating Engaging e-Learning with PowerPoint*. Not only did she capture the essence of the presentation and help me see what my learners perceived as my most important points, but she created an excellent encapsulation of the presentation, which she then broadcast to *her* whole network. My message went much further thanks to her time spent tweeting about it. Note that Cammy created the hashtag #bozbet (for "Bozarth-better"), so her followers could see the tweets all related to the same topic. Part of Cammy's work is shown in Figure 2.6 and is used here with her permission.

Something I had included as a throwaway was a really critical learning point for her. Not only that: she certainly was paying attention! (For Cammy's comments from the whole session, see her LearningVisons blog, August 11, 2009, http://learningvisions.blogspot.com/2009/08/jane-bozarth-better-than-bullet-points.html).

**Figure 2.6. Webinar Backchannel Notes
Created by Cammy Bean**

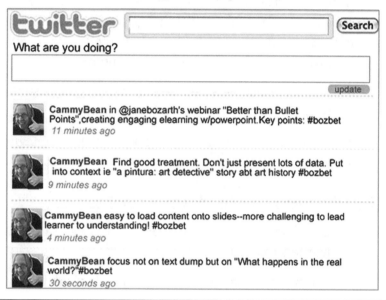

Used with permission.

Intersession Work

Thoughtful use of Twitter can support continued learning between formal class meetings: continuing a conversation from class, sending follow-up comments, and helping learners remain focused and mindful as they work to apply new learning. And it provides a much-needed quick place to get back with that answer you may have promised.

If learners are given takeaway homework, projects, or readings, encourage them to tweet about challenges, what they are learning, tips to share, and new resources. This helps learners become aware of their own learning, helps them to stay on track and in touch with one another, helps you monitor progress, and overall, makes the learning visible. It additionally extends the session beyond the few hours the learners have in class with you, again helping us to get into the spaces between formal events.

Continue Conversations

A frustration shared by learners and instructors alike is the conversation cut short by the end of class time. Continuing conversations can increase retention, and Twitter is an excellent place for that. In the hours following class simply begin with something like:

- Roger was asking about change management strategies in dealing with the IT department. Any suggestions?

- Let's continue our thoughts on marketing strategies targeting a younger workforce.

Other ways of continuing conversations:

- Offer a new question or topic every few days, again encouraging learners to engage with one another.

- Continually ask: "How have you been applying the information from last week's session?"

- "What challenges do you see?" or "What else do you need to know to maximize your learning?"

- Tweet quick reminders about assignments.

- Offer links to interesting articles or websites.

- Use Twitter as an advance organizer, providing information about upcoming topics or course content.

- Encourage learners to follow an expert in the industry (sales, insurance, medical policymaking, etc.) or author. For instance, learners in a leadership course might choose to follow @stephenrcovey or The Leadership Challenge: @TLCTalk.

Talk to an Expert

As the instructor, find an author or industry leader who's a frequent tweeter and ask whether he or she would be willing to take some questions from your class. Ask learners, between sessions, to find an expert or author on Twitter and engage in a brief interview with them, getting their ideas on issues related to the course content.

Even if the course content is proprietary, there's no reason learners can't go out and look for other thought leaders or groups in the same industry to build on what they're learning in your course. For example, if I were teaching on the Truth in Lending Act, I'd have them look for some news stories about lending relevant to the Truth in Lending Act. Or perhaps have them do some research on why we have a Truth in Lending Act. Or share their thoughts on what would happen if there was no Truth in Lending Act.

Tom Kuhlmann, www.articulate.com/rapidelearning

Debate

Set up a debate, with different learners assigned to differing points of view. One of my favorite twists on this is, in management, supervisory, or communication skills training, have learners take the point of view opposite their own. This forces them to spend a few moments trying to see the point of view of another.

Discuss pros and cons of organizations blocking sites like Facebook and YouTube.

Discuss the advantages and disadvantages of offering workers longevity pay.

Role Play

Create a Twitter account, for example, AngryCustomer. Assign learners the role of characters (for instance, one is the customer, another the sales rep, another the district manager, and another a representative from the manufacturing department) and engage in a conversation to resolve an issue around a misplaced shipment or defective item. Figure 2.7 shows an example of a role play used in training by Acme

Figure 2.7. Role Play in Twitter

Industries, a retail computer store. IndiraJay is the customer, AcmeMan
the support tech. Participants are using hashtag #acmanRP4 to separate
this exercise from the public Twitter stream. (Remember to read from
bottom to top.)

- Set up a new fictional hire, who develops as a character like "Jane."
  Create her account ("JaneHire") and give new hires the password to
  the account. Have them post tweets for Jane as their days unfold and
  they encounter issues and resolve problems.

- Or take on the role of "JaneHire" yourself, posting her challenges
  and dilemmas each day. Ask your learners to take on the role of
  managers attempting to help her with the on-boarding process.

Reflections on Articles, Videos, Blog Reviews, or Website Visits

Direct learners to an online reading or handout you have provided by
saying, "Please read the article at www.acme.com" or "Please review the

Douglas reading I attached in an email to you this morning." Then ask them to tweet their responses to one or more of the following. As always, encourage them to engage with and respond to one another:

- What do you know now that you didn't know before?

- What did you find interesting or surprising?

- Did this solve any problem for you? How?

- What did you disagree with?

- What can you do with this information?

- What observations or comments would you like to add?

- What point did you find especially novel or useful?

- What wasn't clear?

- Do you agree or disagree that there is no such thing as ROI in training?

- The article offers ten critical points. How many do you agree/disagree with?

- How does this tie in to our discussion last week?

- How does the Kouzes and Posner leadership model differ from the situational leadership model?

- How can you apply this to your work?

Figure 2.8 shows a tweet asking for reflection on a reading assignment.

Independent Research

Use Twitter to offer opportunities for guided, self-directed research among individuals or teams. For instance:

- Assign each learner a different leadership model to research and discuss.

- Ask each learner to find and post a link to one web-based resource (article, link, blog post, etc.) on the topic or examples of industry

Figure 2.8. Reflection on a Reading Assignment

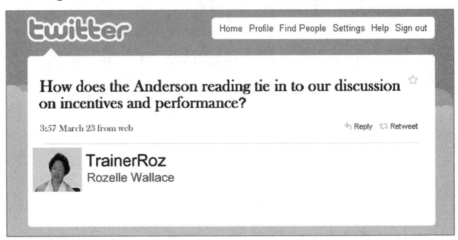

standards. Have them also say why they chose it. (Offer the additional instructions that, once something is posted, it can't be posted by another.)

• Find an expert on the topic and ask him or her to offer a piece of advice for success.

Round Robin

Assign learners numbers. Number 1 asks a question based on course content; number 2 answers it. Then number 2 asks a new question. Number 3 answers that one, and so on. The person with the final number then writes one last question to be answered by number 1.

Brainstorm/Poll

Invite learners to post a quick answer to a question such as "What is one thing you think we could do to improve the customer experience in our stores?" Use one of the twitter polling tools (like www.twtpoll.com) and have participants vote on the best ideas.

Put a question to your learners:

- What do you see affecting sales most in your region?
- What would you say are key moments in the company history?
- What do you think should be modified on the revised JL-784?

Keep Others in the Loop

Learners tweeting from a training class or a conference can provide key points so co-workers who aren't attending can follow along. Also, if your organization takes trainees to offsite locations for long stretches of time, set up a twitter account so spouses, partners, and children can keep with what's going on.

A Singular Use: Foreign Language Instruction

Twitter is ideally suited for quick, real-time practice for learners engaged in workplace foreign language instruction workshops. A Twitter search for "Spanish language practice," for instance, leads to others who share that interest. A little patience will help trainers find Spanish speakers who wish to practice their English with native English speakers wanting to practice their Spanish. Twitter's 140-character, informal nature takes emphasis off of perfect spelling and grammar; learners can *practice* communicating ideas so that they are understood. The tweets themselves are pretty interesting to see, even if you don't read the language:

@dramanimi הבתכ ?םתוא בכעמ וא םייחה תא גרדשמ קדקודמ ימצע דועית
"םיתממכמ"ה לע תנייינעמ

ברשת: דועית ימצע הפקת וד"חותמ מספרייט http://bit.ly.4G76r

@valdis_s Piedalos Jane Bozarth webinārā par sociālo tīklu izmantošanu mācībās. Mans praktiskais atklājums

@jeroenb Vandaag training eLearning, functioneringsgesprek en feed-back masterstudenten

@MariaMachina A mi también. Luego si te toca uno al lado del avión es lo peor, su gordura se pasa a tu asiento.

Formative Evaluation

A good deal of literature in the training field deals with summative evaluation—what happens when the training is over—but little addresses the importance of formative evaluation. This can help the trainer identify what is "sticking," whether learners are taking away the most important information.

- Summarize our discussion of change management strategies.

- Tweet one key point (no repeats) from yesterday's class.

- Tweet one key idea from the Covey reading.

- Conduct an A to Z summary (no repeats). Each learner tweet one thing he or she has learned. Each item should start with a different letter of the alphabet, from A to Z with no repeats. An example is shown in Figure 2.9 (remember to read from bottom to top).

Summative Evaluation

Too often, follow-up evaluation takes the form only of "smile-sheet" rating forms, hastily completed at the end of the session by tired

Figure 2.9. A to Z Class Review

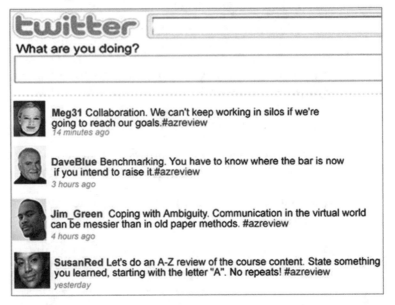

learners anxious to get on the road, go to the restroom, go to lunch, or get back to work. Use Twitter to keep up with after-chat and to gather more meaningful evaluation data once learners are back on the job and working to implement their new skills.

Employ Twitter to conduct one-week, two-week, four-week, and six-month check-ins. For instance, invite discussion around such topics as:

- What activity was most useful for you? Why?
- What are some questions you still have?
- What class material had the most value?
- What will you change/have you changed as a result of the training?
- How can you best maximize your investment in completing this training?

Post-Class: Extending the Life of the Training

Experienced trainers—and experienced learners—have all felt the rush of good intentions as they leave a training experience, only to see it fade and dissipate as the realities of the day-to-day job set in. Twitter is an easy means of helping learners stay in touch with one another and with the trainer, supporting the growth of a learning community and continued development, providing encouragement and support as learners work to apply their new skills, and serving as a vehicle for cultivating a learning community.

As the trainer, you may choose to include only members of a single class, keeping discussions insular, or set up a separate Twitter account for use by everyone who completes the program, thereby growing the community.

Here are some ideas for extending the reach of the training beyond the course itself:

- Provide follow-on coaching to former learners as they implement their learning on the job. Ask how they're doing, provide quick responses, encourage others to answer.

- Offer quick announcements of upcoming company events, new training programs, external workshops and conferences, wellness or career fairs, and local book signings by authors of interest.

- Suggest a group outing to a relevant film.

- Host—or ask learners to host—a Twitter-based book club. Set up an account for the conversation. Take a section or chapter at a time, inviting others to tweet their reactions, comment on new learning and surprising content, and discuss points of agreement or disagreement.

- Occasionally offer an informal "tweet-up," inviting your learners to join you for lunch or coffee at a central location.

- Provide a recommended reading list one tweet at a time.

- Take photos during live sessions; occasionally post one via a Twitter application such as Twitpic as a follow-up to spark memories and remind learners of the training.

- Recommend others for learners to follow.

- Share your own new learning.

- Your organization can't afford to send more than one person to a conference? Have that person tweet key points from the conference sessions. Several people attending the same conference? Ask them to attend different sessions and tweet to share the knowledge.

- Use a free external Twitter application (such as Social Oomph, Twaitter, or Brizzly) to set up timed tweets weeks or months in advance. Post an idea of the week, article or resource of the day, or book recommendation of the month. Tweet questions such as:

  - What are you reading? How is it extending your learning?

  - What is one success you've had in using your new learning?

  - What do you find you still have trouble with?

  - Where do you see disconnects between training and reality? What changes can we make to the training?

Don't feel, as the trainer, that you have to do it all yourself. Encourage participants to lead a conversation or throw out a question to the group, even scheduling such activities if you feel the need.

Twitter Tools

Once you start you'll find there are a number of tools that will make your life as a Twittering trainer easier. Products come and go and change, but as of this writing there are several you might want to explore. These are products offered by outside developers, so try Googling for them. Most link easily to your existing Twitter account.

Tweetdeck is a desktop client with a customizable interface that allows you to manage large numbers of people in your Twitter stream. You can organize them into groups, manage multiple accounts (for instance, if you have a personal Twitter account and another for your leadership course, keep track of hashtag conversations, keep search windows open, and much more. Tweetdeck also integrates with Facebook and LinkedIn so can pull feeds from there as well. Figure 2.10 shows, from left to right, the feed for my own Twitter account, my search for tweets that

Figure 2.10. Tweetdeck Showing Main Account Feed and Results for Two Search Terms

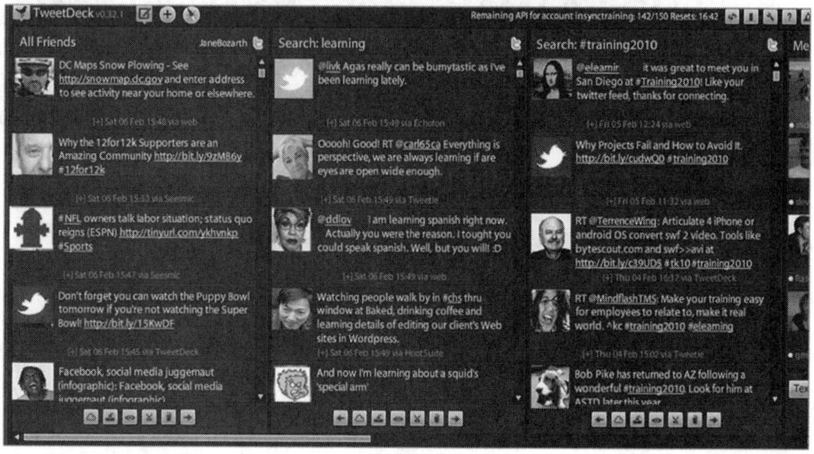

include the word "learning," and my search for tweets related to the Training 2010 conference in San Diego, referenced in tweets as #training2010. Columns are easily rearranged. Figure 2.11 shows the feed for my Twitter account, my LinkedIn network updates, and my Facebook news feed. The Tweetdeck mobile version for smartphones provides identical capabilities and has the same look.

To see which Twitter clients people are using, just look under the tweet. You can then click on the product name to go to the product's site. Figure 2.12 shows a tweet I sent from Tweetie. (*Note:* Tweetie is soon changing its name to "Twitter for iPhone.")

SocialOomph, *Twaitter*, and *Brizzly* are just a few of several available tools that will let you create tweets ahead of time and set the schedule for when they will appear in the timeline. For instance, you can use the tools to auto-tweet a different book title every Tuesday morning at 11 Eastern time.

Figure 2.11. Tweetdeck Can Also Pull Feeds from LinkedIn and Facebook

Figure 2.12. Example of Tweet Sent from Tweetie

Figure 2.13 shows an example of scheduling a tweet in Twaitter for the "Leadership2012" account. The "schedule" button lets you choose when it will appear in your feed.

Multimedia sharing tools provide easy means for uploading media to your Twitter feed. Popular products include *TwitPic* for uploading photos, and *blip.fm* for linking to songs. As already mentioned, *GroupTweet* will allow you to create a private messaging area visible only to groups you create, such as learners in your course. Also mentioned was www.twtpoll.com for creating surveys and polls in Twitter. Figure 2.14 shows a poll created with Twtpoll. The program generates a link for you to include in a tweet. They can then go to the poll.

Respondents can also view the results, as shown in Figure 2.15.

Figure 2.13. You Can Easily Auto-Schedule Tweets

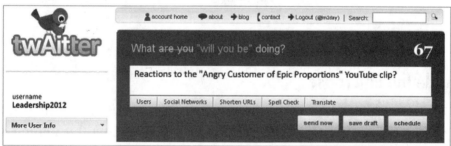

Figure 2.14. Twtpoll Questions

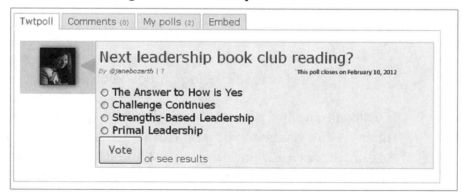

Figure 2.15. Twtpoll Results

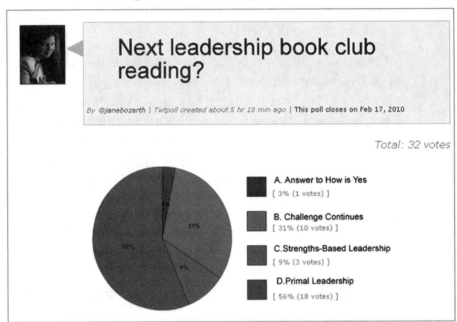

Inside the Enterprise

Organizations with tight security issues—such as banking and law enforcement—may find the openness of Twitter threatening. While that very openness is really the point, there are microblogging tools similar to Twitter that can be restricted to use only within the organization. Currently, the most popular of these is a product called Yammer.

Case: Microblogging at Qualcomm

Qualcomm wanted a private microblogging experience rather than to work via the public nature of Twitter and chose Yammer because it was ready for the enterprise and had a mobile interface. Employees can access it via smartphones, web browsers, RSS feeds, an Outlook plugin, the company's SharePoint server, and even via Twitter. They use Yammer for workplace learning activities— particularly knowledge sharing in the sense of "does anyone know?" discussions and industry updates. But the product is used as well for community building, bridging distances, overcoming silos, internal marketing, and helping individuals increase their sphere of influence. Usage rapidly grew to more than two thousand users. Benefits reported from the initial experiment? Emergence of knowledge experts, new links between former silos like IT, Legal, and HR, and bringing new groups together.

Source: http://elearningweekly.wordpress.com/2009/11/19/a-case-study-of-micro-blogging-for-learning-at-qualcomm.

The U.S. Centers for Disease Control (CDC) uses Twitter to support public education efforts. Here are some examples of tweets sent by the CDC:

Stay healthy! Send family and friends a hand washing eCard: http://is.gd/uL0Z #swineflu Please share!

Access important CDC info including H1N1 flu via the mobile CDC website at http://m.cdc.gov.

Have Swine Flu questions? Please call CDC INFO at 1-800-232-4636 for all health questions. Available in English and Spanish 24/7.

#AAAIDS Act Against AIDS. Every 9.5 minutes, someone is infected with HIV. Learn more: www.nineandahalfminutes.org.

Update 6/3/09: 11,054 cases of novel H1N1 flu, 17 deaths, 52 states/territories affected: http://tr.im/niJR #swineflu.

Links to official H1N1 flu web pages for all 50 states plus DC are available on the CDC website.

Source: http://www.cdc.gov/SocialMedia/Tools/guidelines/pdf/microblogging.pdf.

Summary

I hope by now you've set up a Twitter account and, even better, tried some things out as you followed along with this book. Twitter is a fun tool for generating quick conversation, finding answers, sharing links, broadcasting thoughts, and supporting "chatter" during and after training events. It is less work for learners than trying to keep up with email-chain conversations about, for instance, what everyone is reading. As posting is so informal, there is less pressure for perfect composition, as might be the case with more robust discussion tools. Used as a virtual water cooler, a place to manage conversation and assignments, and a resource for locating expertise, thoughtful use of Twitter in training can be of great benefit to both trainers and learners.

Facebook* and Other Communities

In a Nutshell

Facebook is a single-login site that aggregates many forms of social media, such as messages, photos, videos, events, discussions, and links.

In a Larger Container

Facebook is a one-stop shop that allows users to interact with "friends" of their choosing and participate in groups with other users. Users can post status updates, links, photos, and multimedia such as videos; engage in online games such as word games or the property-amassing FarmVille; take online Facebook-based quizzes; join groups such as those interested in learning French or planning a high school reunion; or subscribe to information posted on fan pages of a favorite TV show, author, or business. The user can choose what content he or she posts that will be available to these friends. For instance, some friends may be allowed to see everything, while others may not have access to photos.

Upon logging in to the site, learners will see a "feed" of friends' activities. Items such as wall posts and pictures will appear on the learner's page in chronological order.

---

*Facebook is a trademark of Facebook, Inc.

How to View Facebook

As little as five years ago, a person wanting to create a web page with pictures, videos, chat features, and discussion boards had to have knowledge of html coding, knowledge of video and photo editing, ftp software to upload the material, and access to server space. Now, on Facebook, users can easily create and customize their own online materials.

"Facebook addicts prefer the social portal model versus having to log in to AIM, Yahoo Messenger, GMail, Hotmail, Flickr, YouTube, MySpace, etc. Instead, Facebook gives them a single alternative to all these applications, with one login and interface to manage their online social interaction needs. This largely explains the explosive growth Facebook continues to experience."

Steve Thornton, www.twitip.com/twitter-versus-facebook

Facebook is an easy-to-use, intuitive tool for instructors. It's good for staying in frequent contact and helps the instructor, training department, or organization build a sense of community. You may choose Facebook for hosting an entire online course, to supplement a classroom-based or blended course, or to provide a space for course graduates or all your organization's learners to engage and share knowledge and ideas.

For instructors, Facebook can in many ways replicate the functions provided by a formal content management system. Use it for communicating assignments, offering reminders, posting notes, providing documents, videos, and slide shows, messaging individuals or groups, hosting online discussions and real-time chats, and scheduling events. As Facebook is already in use by many learners, setup, launch, and learning to use will take less ramp-up time than introducing another tool. Also, since information shows up in the learners' feed, they do not have to go to/log in to your site, page, blog, or learning management system (LMS). Facebook helps you push the information to them, rather than have to work to pull them to some other site.

Finally, Facebook is excellent for drawing people into technology and conversations from which they may have been excluded before. Its informality and user-friendliness make it very accessible to a broad audience and it—more than most other tools—is something of an equalizer/leveler. Learners with lower literacy levels or nonprofessional status, who may be less likely to add a comment to a blog, are perhaps more comfortable adding a short comment to a Facebook wall post or adding a tag to a photo.

Advantages/Disadvantages of Facebook in Training

Advantages

Facebook promotes conversation and can help to reduce the space and power issues between instructor and learners; it helps to "level" the relationships and can support inter-learner interaction rather than just back-and-forth learner-instructor discourse often seen in traditional instruction. Even new users can quickly see the fun and value in connecting with old friends and family members. Facebook is a "sticky" technology, pulling people in and back in as they check on their friends' updates, play FarmVille, continue conversations they've been engaged in, and check back to see whether anyone has made comments on things they have posted themselves. Facebook is undeniably popular, with two hundred million people checking in to their accounts at least once a day. It is therefore likely familiar to and comfortable for many of your learners.

Facebook can substitute for a formal course management system such as Blackboard or Moodle, or even for a corporate LMS. Unlike other systems, Facebook will push instructor, group, or page updates to the learner's Facebook news feed; also, instructors can subscribe to Facebook updates via an RSS feed and will therefore receive updates as they occur, without having to log in at all. This is a distinct advantage over many other content management or LMS systems, which require frequent login.

One of the reasons for Facebook's popularity is that it is so user-friendly. A click or two allows for frequent status updates, uploading photos, linking to videos, and sharing ideas. Many learners will already be using

Facebook, so the trainer incorporating it into his or her practice can put the instruction where learners already live. Learners do not need to access other sites to reach the instructor or access instructional materials; they do not need to keep up with additional passwords or URLs. Effective use of Facebook in instruction supports peer-to-peer interactions and the development of digital literacy skills.

Disadvantages

If ever technology has placed a "shiny object" in the path of an employee, it is probably Facebook. Often viewed by organizations as a timewaster, users—especially new ones—are prone to be seduced by distractors such as games. A challenge of living in the "information age" is dealing with the endless and sometimes overwhelming amount of content thrown at us every day. As with other tools, individuals using Facebook will need to learn to manage the time spent there, especially if using it on work time.

Why Facebook Instead of Something Else?

Facebook's one-stop, one-login nature gives it the advantage over many other tools, such as a blog or separate LMS. The discussion and chat features allow for more robust conversation than Twitter and less post-and-respond back-and-forth between learners and instructor than a blog. Again, many learners are already using Facebook and are very comfortable moving around within it, so it would require less introduction time than many other tools.

Why Facebook in Addition to Something Else?

For organizations using Moodle, Blackboard, or a commercial LMS, Facebook can prove complementary by offering a collaborative, social space; many Facebook applications interface well with these other products. For instance, Facebook users can link their accounts with the Skype instant-messaging and VoIP (voice over internet protocol) telephony services.

Getting Started

Set Up an Account

You will need a valid email address to begin. Then simply visit www
.facebook.com to start the account setup process.

Create a Profile

Facebook will prompt you to create a profile and then walk you through
the process. This is where you decide what and how much to reveal
about yourself: Your employer, marital status, education, even things
like favorite books, movies, or quotes. It is important that you spend
some time learning to use Facebook's privacy settings in order to control
who has access to what you are posting.

Begin Inviting Learners ("Friends")

From within Facebook send your learners invitations to be your "friend."
You can do this directly with learners who are already Facebook users by
using the "send a friend request" feature, or via requests to their email
accounts. *Important:* Instructors using Groups or Fan Pages may invite
participants without having to become their "friends" or vice versa. They
can then fully participate in the group or page without everyone being
privy to their own (or your) personal pages.

Create Friend Lists

You can group your friends into lists. You can then interact with these
lists directly, message only them, etc. As an instructor, you may choose,
for example, to organize your learners into lists according to the course
in which they are currently enrolled, then move them to a list for
course graduates later.

Refine Your Basic Profile into a Limited Profile

Once you have established a profile, acquired friends, and organized
them into lists, you would be well advised to go back and create a

limited profile. The limited profile will allow you to decide who sees what. To create a limited profile:

Click "Profile" at the top of the Facebook page, then "Settings > Privacy Settings."

Choose individual items, such as "Personal Info" or "Photos" and click "customize," as shown in Figure 3.1.

Clicking "customize" will open a new window. You can then choose who can or can't see items, as shown in Figure 3.2.

You can also set up different Facebook accounts for different purposes. I have a personal account to connect with people who really are my "friends" and a business account ("Jane Bozarth Bozarthzone," if you'd like to join me there) for business contacts. I tend to think of it as

Figure 3.1. Facebook Limited Profile Settings

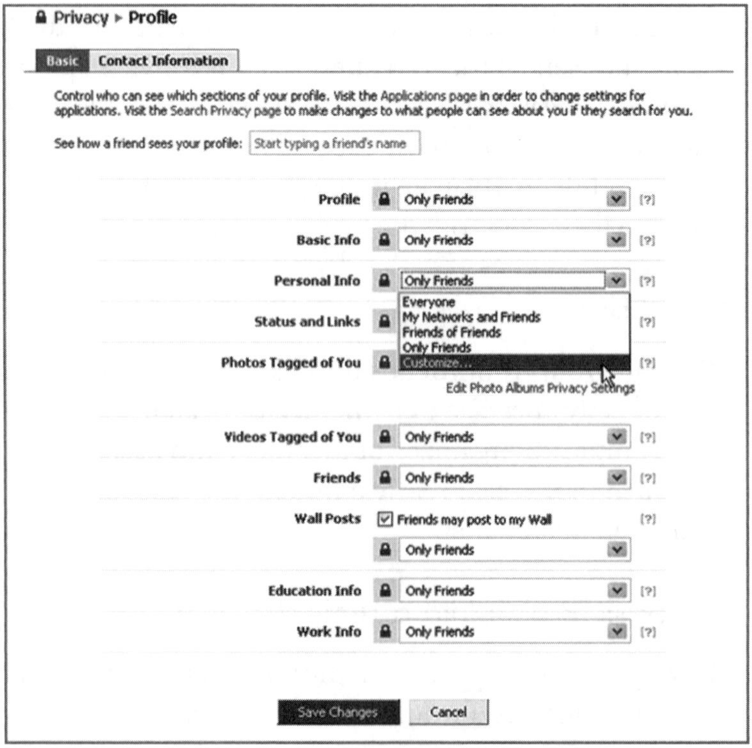

Figure 3.2. Facebook Settings: Choose Who Sees What

having different personas. The "personal Jane" wears jeans and t-shirts, talks about movies and restaurants, and posts pictures of her dog and her husband's Halloween costume. The "business Jane" posts links to research, feeds new information to past class participants, and shares links to educational videos. But "she" doesn't mention her home life, dog, or husband there. You will need different email addresses to create different Facebook accounts. Hotmail, Yahoo Mail, or Gmail accounts are free and work fine for this.

Decide How You Will Use Facebook for Instructional Purposes

Do you want to host an entire class, or provide a space in which learners can communicate in between formal class meetings? Do you want to establish a group site for all the graduates of your flagship leadership program? Do you want to create a learning space for all your organization's employees?

Apart from your personal account page, you can set yourself up as administrator of a group or a fan page. These will provide a separate space for posting information, sharing photos or videos, hosting discussions, etc. Information Groups and pages will also allow you to message all members at once. At present Facebook is still tweaking these and they are becoming more and more alike. For the sake of clarity and space, what follows is a good bit of detail about setting up a group, then a smaller bit about pages and when to choose which. The setup and function are similar and, as with initial setup, Facebook makes the process of creating a group or fan page quite easy. *Important:* People can join a group or fan page without having to set up a "friend" relationship with you or one another.

Create a Group

To create a group, just type "groups" into the Facebook search box. You'll be taken to a new page with a button, "Create a new group." From there you'll edit permissions, stating whether your group members can, for instance, upload photos. Figure 3.3 shows the template for customizing your group.

Then you can invite your learners to join your group. You can choose from among your existing Facebook friends or invite learners by email (see Figure 3.4).

Fan Pages

As this book was going to press, Facebook was still working to iron out the features of groups and fan pages; it's entirely likely that soon the differences will be minimal, or perhaps one type will simply win out over the other. At present, however, there are a few things to consider about pages (as compared to groups):

Figure 3.3. Facebook Groups Allow for Customization

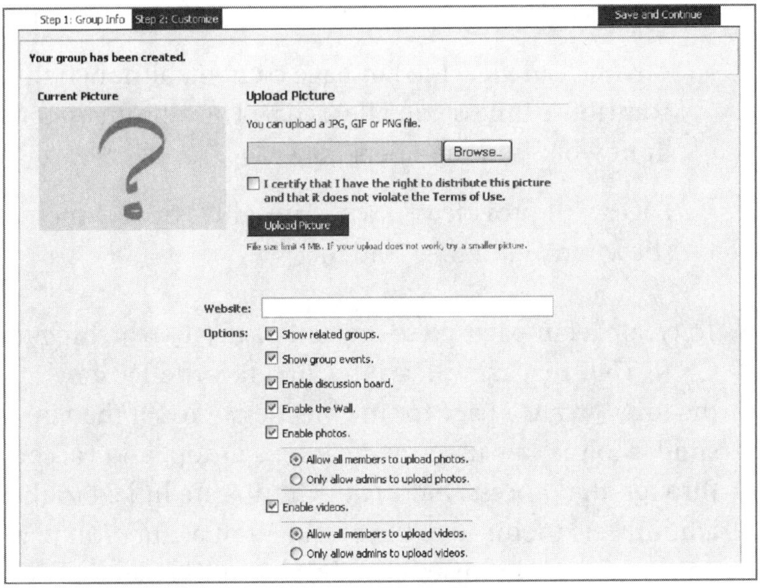

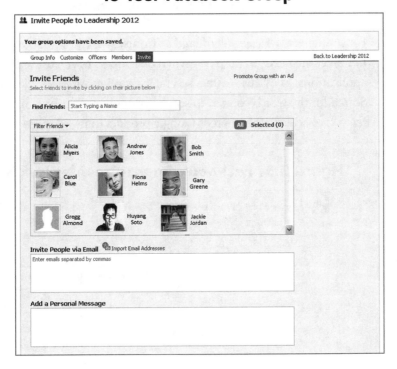

Figure 3.4. Invite "Friends" (and Others) to Your Facebook Group

- Pages will let you add applications, such as notes or polls. At present, groups come with only "photos" "discussions," and "events."

- Anyone can view the fan page content, although they cannot edit or contribute unless you allow that. The administrator of a group can limit what non-members may view.

- Pages will provide you with "insights" or user metrics like the ones shown in Figures 3.5 and 3.6.

To create a fan page, go to any fan page (try searching for something like CNN, *Time* magazine, learning, or a favorite TV show). Scroll down to the link "create a page for my business." You'll then be taken to a page similar to the one used for creating a group, and Facebook will walk you through the process. *Important:* Groups are linked to the person who administers them—like the president of a club. Fan pages do not list the names of the administrators. Think of this essentially as the difference between your own private group and a corporate entity.

Can't I Just Have a Course?

For several years, Facebook offered a "Courses" application but found it did not meet the needs of users. It invited developers to create their own "course" applications; as of this writing, several exist, all in various stages of maturity. Search for the word "course" to see the current applications, and read user reviews to see whether there is a single product that will meet all your needs.

Figure 3.5. Facebook Pages Provide User Metrics

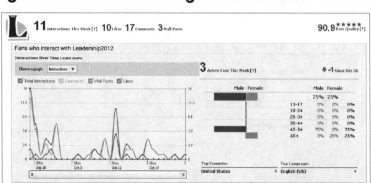

Figure 3.6. More Facebook User Metrics

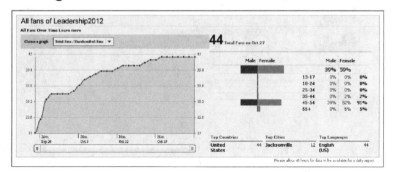

Once Your Personal Page, Group, or Fan Page Is Set Up

Post Messages via the Wall

The top of your Facebook screen will always contain an empty box into which you can enter text. You can also use a drop-down menu there to add a link, a photo, an event, or a video. For an instructor, Wall posts (as shown in Figure 3.7) might include things like daily updates, a reminder about reading assignments, a preview of the upcoming class session, a link to an article, or a YouTube video.

Post Messages Via Private Messages

Facebook allows you to send private messages to individuals, or to message an entire group or list, or all fans at once. These will be delivered to the other person's Facebook inbox.

Create an Event

Learners will receive notification of events, essentially, things with a set time and place: a formal class meeting, a live Facebook chat session, a gathering at a local coffee shop, or a reading by an author at a local library. On your own page you can simply use the drop-down menu shown in Figure 3.8. If you are using a group, you can create an event, invite particular people, ask for RSVPs, etc., as shown in Figure 3.9.

Figure 3.7. Wall Posts Allow for Text and Other Material

Figure 3.8. Creating an Event in Facebook

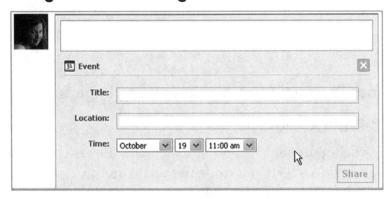

Figure 3.9. Choose Specifics About the Event

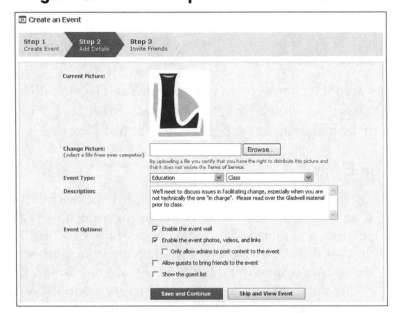

Post a Video

Facebook will let you (and your learners, if you choose) load some video formats onto your wall (or that of your group or fan page). YouTube will generate an URL for you to paste in. You can also upload video you have created on your computer or sent from your cell phone.

Post Documents and PowerPoint Shows (Using an External Application)

If it is only a page or so, and formatting isn't important, you may just choose to paste it into a message or onto the wall. If you are using a fan page, you can add it as a note, an application that can be added to the page that allows learners to open and read it.

For something longer or more formal, or for which formatting matters, you may want to use an external source for posting documents. The free Google documents feature ("Google Docs"), for instance, will allow you to upload documents, including spreadsheets and PowerPoint presentations, and set permissions for learners to view or edit them. If you just want learners to view the document, Google Docs will generate an URL so you can simply share the link in a Facebook wall post. Visit google.com for details.

Google Docs will allow you to post PowerPoint shows that your learners can view or download. SlideShare.net is another popular free site for sharing PowerPoint and will, as with Google Docs, generate a link for you.

Post Photos

The age of digital photography, and the commonality of cell phones with cameras, make taking and posting photos a fairly simple task. You (and your learners, if you choose to let them) can load photos onto your Facebook group or page. These can include photos taken during formal class meetings or photos that reveal something personal about the learner. Consider, also, how to use photos relevant to particular course content, such as pictures of pieces of equipment or demonstrations of effective versus ineffective body language for a sales opening. Photos can be organized into albums; it is easy to add captions and to add "tags" to specify individuals' names.

Engage in Live Chat

Facebook comes with a live chat feature; at present, this allows for chatting only with one other person. As Facebook evolves, it is entirely possible that group chats will become available. As an instructor, the live chat tool could serve as a place for you to host virtual office hours during which you are available "live" to talk with learners.

Host a Discussion

Facebook groups and fan pages come with a discussion board. You or your learners can start, lead, facilitate, and engage in a text-based discussion on course material and other topics of interest. The discussion board can also be used for debates and role plays.

Hosting an Online Course

A Facebook group or fan page can serve as a site for an online course. (Facebook in its early days had a "Courses" application, but found it was not meeting user needs so handed the idea off to individual application developers. At present there is no one standard courses application, and many that exist are geared more toward college students sharing textbooks and working toward grades.) By combining use of the wall to share material such as readings, links, and videos, using available tools to create learning activities (such as the example of having learners conduct an environmental scan and post photos, as shown in figure 3.11), and providing provocative discussion topics and good facilitation of conversation, Facebook can support a robust, interesting online learning experience. Figure 3.10 shows an example of a "Leadership" course.

Wall posts offer contributions from both instructors and class members and include links to articles, book recommendations, and learner blog

Figure 3.10. Leadership Course Hosted in Facebook

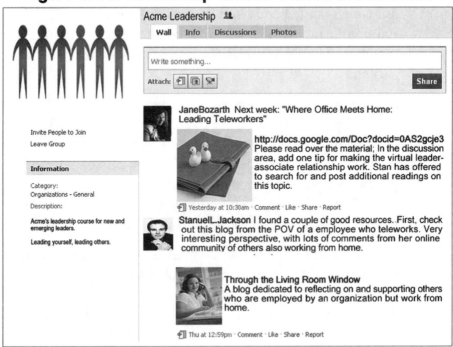

posts. Discussion questions, geared toward the goals of this course, include things like:

- What makes a good leader?

- Are leaders born or made?

- Who has influenced you most as a leader? Why? What can you do to emulate that?

- What is your role in sustaining a work team?

- Discuss a change you attempted that went badly. In retrospect, what could you have done differently?

Trainers, especially those new to working in an online environment, may need to develop some skill at facilitating online discussions. A good discussion starts with a good question, one that leads to conversation rather than just an answer (consider what you know about using open-ended and closed-ended questions). Sometimes discussions stall, requiring the trainer to make a comment to jump-start it; sometimes discussions go off-topic, requiring the trainer to rein them back in.

Learners who are new to this may need some help. Patti Shank's *The Online Learning Idea Book* (2007) offers a list of ideas for helping learners understand what constitutes a good discussion post: Show that you are reading others' comments by referring to them in your own posts; construct an argument, offering evidence and supporting resources; remember that a good post is one that gets people thinking and makes them want to reply.

Leverage Facebook's tools to enhance the learning experience. Learners could, for instance, be asked to post photos or video to the group or page as part of the training experience. As an example, one of my frustrations as a trainer is dealing with the reality of a work culture that does not match the behavior management it is asking learners to develop. A favorite activity, outlined in Kouzes, Posner, and Bozarth's *The Challenge Continues* (2010) invites learners to conduct an environmental scan. Ask them to consider: What does your physical environment say about your organization's culture? Does it support or conflict with stated goals? For instance, if your mission statement says, "All employees are equal partners," then why are there executive parking spaces? Direct learners to take photos of furniture, office space, waiting areas, and signage—whatever is in the work environment—and create a photo album representing their environmental scan. The results can sometimes be surprising. Figure 3.11 shows examples of real cell-phone-camera photos taken by learners during a customer service training course. The organization, purveyor of a large chain of motels and fuel stations, held "respect for customers" as a core value. Do the examples of signage shown support that value? What is the message being sent to customers? What tone has the organization (perhaps inadvertently) set before the customer even sees an employee?

Figure 3.11. Learner-Provided Photos Reveal a Good Deal About Company Culture

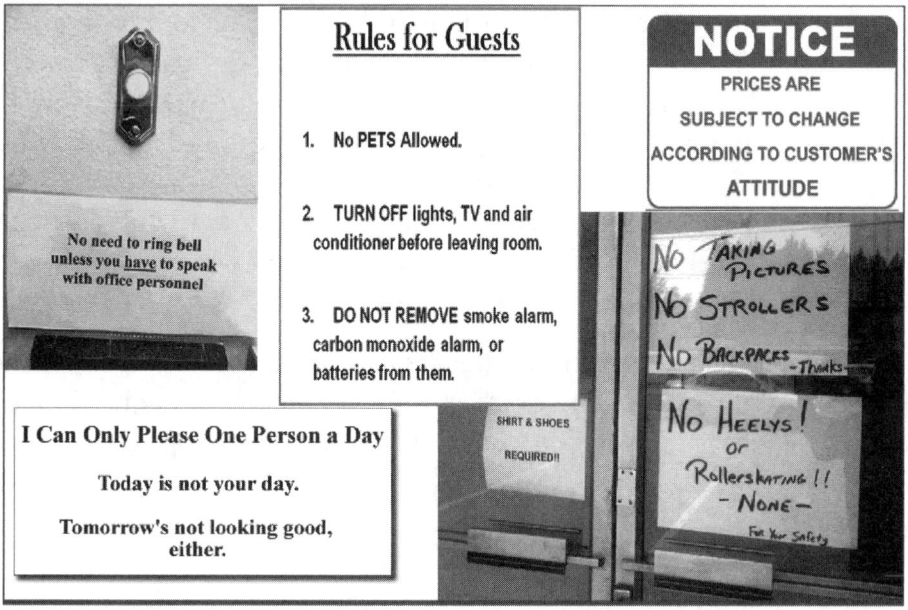

Supplementing a Traditional Class

Facebook provides opportunities and space for more robust discussion than Twitter. Chapter 2 on Twitter outlined small, specific suggestions for questions or topics that would be manageable within Twitter's 140-character limit and rapid-fire, nonlinear style. Many of the ideas would work equally well as Facebook wall posts or discussion questions, while allowing for more conversational depth and organization.

Prior to Course Start

Here are some ideas for using Facebook prior to a course:

- Use Facebook as an advance planner for learners: Post agendas, objectives, links to source texts, etc. This will set the stage for learning and clarify course content for learners.

- Ask learners to read and comment on an article dealing with course content.

- Invite learners to introduce themselves, including an interesting tidbit or two, a photo of their cubicles, or links to a favorite book for sale on Amazon. Remember the old icebreaker-type introductions that included finding "something in your wallet that represents you or your style as a leader or your attitude toward change"? That could easily be replicated by taking photos of items and posting them on Facebook with a sentence or two about why the item was chosen. Figure 3.12 shows an example.

- Offer comments on the upcoming program: Their experience in the topic, their interest in enrolling in the course, a question they'd like to have answered in class, or something they hope others can help with.

Instructor Cristine Clark uses Facebook quizzes, such as the Facebook version of the "Myers-Briggs Type Instrument" or an "Emotional Intelligence" quiz to generate discussion. While the Facebook versions are usually abbreviated versions of full instruments, they are enough to formulate discussion around key ideas. For instance, learners can explore awareness that we all have different experiences, preferences, and ways of responding to situations, and that, essentially, we all have different way of understanding the world.

**Figure 3.12. Facebook Can Support Learner
"Icebreaker" Activities**

Intersession Work

A Facebook group or page can serve as a spot to continue conversation cut short by class time. If the course is structured around set meeting times, use Facebook to keep learners engaged—and keep the learning going—between gatherings. Utilize approaches that will help learners become more mindful of their own learning, stay on track and in touch with one another, and help to reinforce new learning when the learner is back at the worksite.

- Post links to readings, videos, and slideshows. These can include videos of yourself and other instructors, PowerPoint shows, standalone tutorials, or YouTube videos.

- Post an outline of upcoming topics to think about. Ask learners for reactions, reflections, and ideas for applying information.

- Create events to remind learners of project or reading due dates.

- Continually ask, via a wall post or discussion question, "How have you been applying the information from last week's class session?"

- Follow up training sessions with specific questions about applying learning: "Last week we talked about the Pareto Principle. What examples of that have you seen since then?"

- Start separate discussion topics on different pieces of the content. For instance, in a business insurance course, use four different questions to ask learners to provide examples of the four different types of loss exposure: external, internal, governmental, and legal.

- Continue conversations cut short by the end of class time: "Jan was asking for suggestions on establishing herself as credible when she is so much younger than all her employees. What ideas do you have for her?" "Just as we were wrapping up, Nigel asked about the negative aspects of change. How can we address this honestly in selling change to leadership, without undermining our chances at a successful pitch?"

- Use the discussion feature to create a debate ("Jim, Your position is that learners are born, not made. Shana, you believe that everyone

has innate leadership talent that must be nurtured and developed.")
or role play: "Pedro, you are the district sales manager. Alima, you're
the regional sales rep. Sahana, you supervise the customer service
center, which works mostly from an online chat tool. And Xuan, you
are the customer. Xuan has been promised delivery of a product
that's now been delayed for a third time. He's already spoken with
customer care twice. He is angry and his message has been kicked up
to Sahana."

- Use the discussion feature to host a "meet the expert" conversation.
  This could be someone from within the company, an author, or
  other expert in the field.

- Use the discussion feature to invite assigned "varied reactions." Ask
  learners to respond to video clips, articles, or news stories from
  various perspectives. Assign learners (or groups of learners) roles
  such as the naysayer, the one who believes anything, the devil's
  advocate, the detective (lots of questions), the disagreer, the person
  who can't take a stand, and the one who takes everything at face
  value—seeing no context beyond the immediate issue.

- "Hot Seat": Assign learners to groups and a date (a specific day, or
  week, when it will be their turn to be in the "hot seat"). Provide each
  group with a piece of content, theme, or issue from the course
  content for which they will be responsible. They need to research
  and read material (either that you provide or instruct them to access
  via web or other searches), collect links or other resources, and
  essentially educate themselves. They will then be in the 'hot seat' to
  answer questions, facilitate conversations, and so forth during their
  time slots.

- Create "critical incident" discussions: "Describe a time you were
  able to apply consensus-building techniques when leading a work
  team." "Describe a time when you were able to put your knowledge
  of the NC-8732D training to work in resolving a manufacturing
  delay."

- Use a photo as a touch point to spark discussion. During a course
  on preparing social workers for home visits, for instance, offer a

photo like the one in Figure 3.13 and ask: "What are some safety concerns here?" (Some possible answers: high heels, large bag, talking on phone.) Further facilitate the discussion by asking learners to generate their own tips for safe practices during home visits.

Facebook can also provide the instructor with evaluation data. Discussion comments can reveal whether, and how much, of the training seems to be "sticking," whether there appear to be learning gaps, and the extent to which learners are working to apply new learning to the work setting. This can serve both to further support individuals enrolled in the particular course sessions and to refine future offerings.

Figure 3.13. Visual Prompt for Learner Activity

Building a Learning Community with Facebook

As many learners already use Facebook and check in frequently, and as items posted on a group or page wall will appear in the learner's feed, Facebook offers an excellent vehicle for "getting into the spaces" between formal learning events. Consider creating group or fan pages for graduates of particular courses or topics of interest to a broad span of your learners. For instance, "building and sustaining change," "preparing for management," or "strategies for continual improvement."

Invite employees (not only your "trainees") to participate in Facebook groups focused on a topic of special interest in your organization. Including all staff helps to build stronger ties to the training department. Post articles, videos, and other references. Encourage conversation about the topic. Use Facebook to foster

Figure 3.14. Ethics Discussion Hosted on Facebook

informal one-time mentoring by a staff member to an employee via a comment or suggestion. Figure 3.14 shows an example of a discussion held by employees participating in an "ethics" Facebook group hosted by the training shop, which also offers ethics workshops several times a year.

Case: Facebook as a Community for InSync Training, LLC, Course Graduates

Jennifer Hofmann's InSync Training, LLC (www.insynctraining. com and www.insynctraining-eu.com) specializes in training facilitators and designers who will be working in synchronous, virtual classroom environments, such as Elluminate, WebEx, Adobe Connect, and iLinc. She offers several multi-session certificate programs in synchronous facilitation and design, typically with some twelve to eighteen learners in each. On course evaluations, graduates reported time and time again that they wanted a space in which they could talk about their new practice, discuss their growth, share tips, and work through one another's challenges. InSync set up a Facebook group as a space for the graduates. The community manager created an initial plan:

- Membership would be open to anyone who wished to join, but members would be actively recruited only from the pool of practitioners who had completed InSync courses. The group was not meant to serve everyone who had ever attended a webinar.

- Several discussion topics were set up around course content. These would serve as conversation starters, but members would be encouraged to start their own new topics.

- A library of relevant articles and links was developed for distribution to the group across a span of time (in order to have fresh content at the ready).

- The community manager would do a quick recap of group activities and send a message to all members once a week to pull members back to the group. This message is not sent according to a set schedule, making it routine, but comes out at a different day and time each week. Messages to members are kept to a minimum to avoid engendering a feeling that messages are spam.

Over the span of several months, the group grew to 350 members from all over the world, mostly from the pool of InSync Training's course graduates. The five initial discussion topics quickly tripled as participants started their own, on subjects ranging from opinions about software to strategies for dealing with multicultural audiences in the live-online setting. Past participants were able to reconnect with friends from courses they'd taken; synchronous trainers and designers feeling isolated in their roles found many others who shared their interests. Perhaps best of all, graduates—most of whom were new practitioners—were able to continue the discussions from their own training as they worked to transfer their new learning to the workplace. Member Greg Sweet says: "It is the community I was looking for."

Readers are invited to visit the group: Go to Facebook and search for "InSync Training."

Going Mobile

Facebook offers a free mobile application for smartphones that offer functionality similar to that offered on the full site. Users can update status, comment on another's status, and post photos and videos. At the present time Facebook mobile allows for interacting with fan pages, but not groups. Figure 3.15 shows an example of a Facebook class page displayed on an iPhone.

**Figure 3.15. Facebook Class Page Accessed
via Mobile Application**

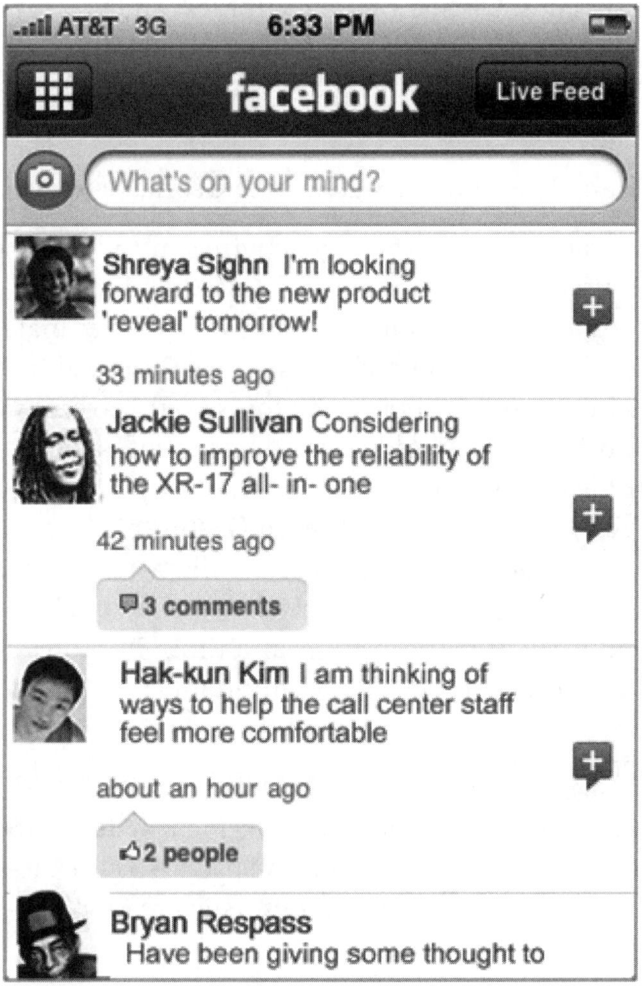

And Now, a Few Words about LinkedIn

Whenever I speak on using Facebook in training, someone invariably asks about LinkedIn, alleging that it is the "professional" version of Facebook. It is a place for people to connect, often on a purely professional level, without photos of kids or distracting games. But overall, similarities between Facebook and LinkedIn are few. You can set up groups, invite members and manage memberships, and host private discussions. Discussions allow for text and pasted-in links. As some LinkedIn members choose to have hundreds or even thousands of contacts, you can (much like Twitter) choose from among them a smaller list of contacts to "follow."

Figures 3.16 through 3.20 illustrate some of the basics of LinkedIn.

For training purposes, any activities in this book involving basic text discussions can be adapted for use in a LinkedIn group. Links to external sites, documents, videos, and other materials can be pasted into the discussion messages. As I mentioned in the Introduction, it's important to choose the tools your learners will use. A 2009 Deloitte report stated that 47 percent of Baby Boomers maintain a profile on a social site. Of those, 73 percent are Facebook users, while 13 percent use LinkedIn (Deloitte, 2009). Individuals in certain professions may be more likely to be on LinkedIn, particularly jobseekers, those in need of making sales or developing vendor-client relationships, and those in professions for whom a broad contact base can be important.

Other Communities

Some learning or content management systems (LMSs, LCMSs) are now working to include community spaces, so check to see whether a product your organization uses—such as Moodle—includes something

Figure 3.16. You Can Choose People and Discussions to Follow

Figure 3.17. One-Page Setup for Creating a LinkedIn Group

Figure 3.18. Invite People to Your Group by Choosing Among Your Connections or Sending to an Email List

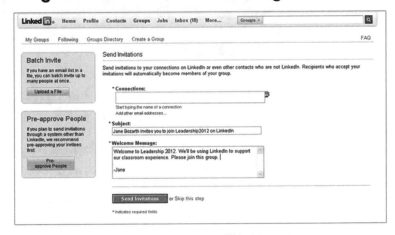

you might consider using. There are also a number of free online communities that provide for functionality similar to that offered by Facebook. They can provide a separate, private space for learners to engage. In choosing to use one of these, remember that they require from your learners setting up another account, keeping up with another

Figure 3.19. LinkedIn Groups and Subgroups Are Places to Host Discussions

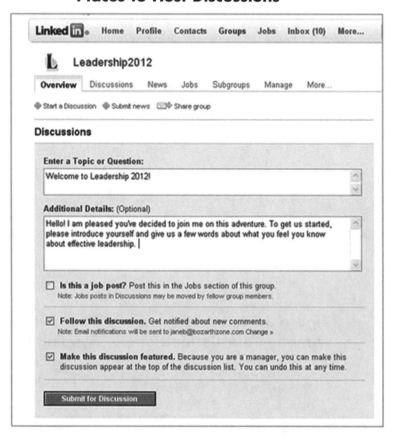

Figure 3.20. Discussion Topics Appear on the LinkedIn Group Site

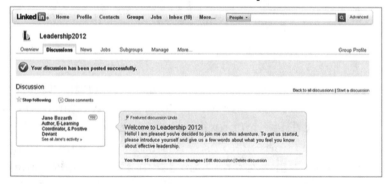

login, and remembering to check in. If learners are already checking in to Facebook, LinkedIn, or your organization's LMS, you might want to look for ways of utilizing that product rather than ask learners to keep up with yet one more site.

One such online community provider is Ning (www.ning.com), a site that allows individuals, schools, or businesses to create their own social networks. Members can join communities and participate in discussions, contribute to blogs, share photos and videos, and so forth. Pages and community sites are highly customizable, with easy-change templates and widgets. Members of communities create their own home pages and share their own ideas and materials. Figure 3.21 shows the Ning home

Figure 3.21. Ning Community Member Home Page

The image is used courtesy of Patty Ball and Ning.

page for Patti Ball, a member of the Northeast (USA) SABES Tech trainings community. She has chosen widgets for sharing her documents, video tutorials, and bookmarks with other members of the NESABES Ning community.

As this book went into print production, Ning announced it would discontinue its free group/network hosting service. Users wishing to stay with Ning will need to upgrade to premium accounts, starting at US $10 per month. As noted elsewhere, technologies and products are ever-evolving, but as of this writing some free alternatives to Ning include Cubetree, Jabbster, Shout'em, and EdModo. Wordpress bloggers have access to BuddyPress, which requires a bit more technical skill than the others products. Depending on the functionality desired by users, old message-board-based standbys like Yahoo Groups and Google groups are still available as well.

Summary

Allowing for more length than Twitter, without the formality of a blog or the required-contribution feel of a wiki, Facebook or other communities can prove an effective tool for supporting instructional goals. Learners are given one-login access to a wealth of collaborative, engaging materials and activities; instructors, a one-stop space for hosting web materials from links and photos to videos and discussions.

Blogs

In a Nutshell

A blog (shortened from "weblog") provides an online space for posting chronologically ordered comments or ideas that can include text, photo, video, audio, and links to other sites, blogs, or documents. Readers can respond to posted content.

In a Larger Container

A blog is an easy, one-stop, do-it-yourself web page creation tool. Most blogging tools are easy to use, give a professional look, and allow for adding images and multimedia. The blog software also provides for simple for post-and-respond interaction. Readers wishing to receive updates can subscribe to your blog via an RSS feed (see Key Terms in the Introduction for details on RSS).

Blogs in general provide an experience that is somewhat less "connected" than do technologies such as Twitter and Facebook. There is typically less one-to-one or casual interaction. Rather than create lists of friends or followers, simply give your learners a link to the blog. If you are asking learners to create and update their own blogs, then everyone will need the links to everyone else's blogs.

How to View Blogs

In their early days, blogs acquired a reputation as a place for one-person rants. But apart from their functionality as an easy web page creation tool, blogs provide an excellent space for reflection, post-and-response conversation, and knowledge sharing. For the instructor looking for course architecture, a blog is a clean, simple space for arranging assignments, discussion questions, and links to course material.

A blog can even be used to host an entire online course. Here are screenshots from the flagship example, "23 Things," created by Helene Blowers for use by library staff. Wanting to help staff become more comfortable with using new technologies, Helene used a free blogging tool to set up a site outlining a course lasting eight and a half weeks, during which learners were guided through twenty-three assignments. These provided walk-throughs of one technology at a time. "23 Things" may represent the perfect marriage of instruction and technology. Blowers created a program that uses social media to teach social media.

The "23 Things" assignments were simply listed one after another, with links to more detail on the blog main page. This is shown in Figure 4.1.

An example is "Week 3: Photos & Images," which links to the full lesson. This is also placed on the blog and includes images, audio notes from the instructor, instructions for exploring the topic, and details about the associated assignment, as shown in Figure 4.2.

Advantages/Disadvantages of Blogs in Training

Advantages

Blogs are free, easy to create and update, and provide simple tools for adding links, photos, and videos. Most blog sites offer options for audio and video posting, and some provide capability for calling in from a telephone. Blog posts can be created ahead of time and scheduled for upload to the web. Instructors can obtain metrics about blog use, such as number of views or the time of day/day of week for views. Blogs can be password-protected and viewable only to those to whom the instructor gives access. While you can restrict access to the blog, those working for companies concerned about security or privacy can pay to

Figure 4.1. "23 Things" Assignments
on One Blog Page

Listed below are 23 Things (or small exercises) that you can do on the web to explore and expand your knowledge of the Internet and Web 2.0. Staff are encouraged to complete all 23 items on this list by October 31st in order to to receive a free USB/MP3 player. Those staff that complete all items by October 6th will also qualify for the laptop drawing and other prizes that will be awarded on All Staff Day.

23 Learning 2.0 Things*
(Note: Details about each task will be activated every week with posts related to each item)

Week 1: Introduction (official start of week August 7th)
1.   Read this blog & find out about the program.
2.   Discover a few pointers from lifelong learners and learn how to nurture your own learning process.

Week 2: Blogging
3.   Set up your own blog & add your first post.
4.   Register your blog on PLCMC Central and begin your Learning 2.0 journey.

Week 3: Photos & Images
5.   Explore Flickr and learn about this popular image hosting site.
6.   Have some Flickr fun and discover some Flickr mashups & 3rd party sites.
7.   Create a blog post about anything technology related that interests you this week.

Week 4: RSS & Newsreaders
8.   Learn about RSS feeds and setup your own Bloglines newsreader account.
9.   Locate a few useful library related blogs and/or news feeds.

Week 5: Play Week
10.   Play around with an online image generator.
11.   Take a look at LibraryThing and catalog some of your favorite books.
12.   Roll your own search tool with Rollyo.

Week 6: Tagging, Folksonomies & Technorati
13.   Learn about tagging and discover a Del.icio.us (a social bookmaking site)
14.   Explore Technorati and learn how tags work with blog posts.
15.   Read a few perspectives on Web 2.0, Library 2.0 and the future of libraries and blog your thoughts.

Week 7: Wikis

"23 Things" image used with permission of Helene Blowers.

Figure 4.2. Assignments Are Linked to Additional Details

#5 Discover Flickr

Listen to this podcast [2:38]--> ▶ [⬤────] 00:00:00   powered by ODEO

Photo sharing websites have been around since the 90s, but it took a small startup site called Flickr to catapult the idea of "sharing" into a full blown online community. Within the past year, Flickr has become the fastest growing photo sharing site on the web and is known as one of the first websites to use keyword "tags" to create associations and connections between photos and users of the site.

For this discovery exercise, you are asked to take a good look at Flickr and discover what this site has to offer. Find out how tags work, what groups are, and all the neat things that people and other libraries (list also here) are using Flickr for.

Chalkboard bookshelves
Originally uploaded by hblowers.

Discovery Resources:

- Flickr Learn More tour **(6 steps)**
- Mediamazine Flickr Tutorials
- Flickr: Popular tags
               Interesting- Last 7 days
- Flickr Services **(3rd party applications & mashups)**
  and let's not forget to look at some other libraries on Flickr

Discovery Exercise:

In this discovery exercise, you have two options...

a.   Take a good look around Flickr and discover an interesting image that you want to blog about. Be sure to include either a link to the image or, if you create a Flickr account, you can use Flickr's blogging tool to add the image in your post. Another option you have for including images in your post is to use Blogger's photo upload tool.

"23 Things" image used with permission of Helene Blowers.

have blogs placed inside the company firewall. Finally, unlike with many LMSs, instructors can use the blog settings to be notified by email whenever a comment is made to a blog post.

Disadvantages

Blogs are easy to start but more challenging to sustain. Blog posts typically are longer than, for instance, comments on Twitter or Facebook, and the blog may seem more formal to learners. While blogs allow for use of multimedia and varied approaches, it is easy to fall into using them for long comments or writing assignments, which may prove challenging to weaker writers or to busy learners.

Why Blogs Instead of Something Else?

Where the microblogging tool Twitter provides a mechanism for quick-and-short messaging, blogs invite somewhat longer responses and can support deeper reflection, discussion of pros/cons, analysis, and application of critical thinking. It is somewhat more formal and less cluttered than other technologies discussed in this book and may for some instructors provide a space in which they feel they have more control. It is easier to "contain" the course within the blog than it might be with a product like Facebook or Twitter, both prone to presenting myriad distractions for learners. Also, unlike Twitter or Facebook, blogs provide archiving, usually by month, and are searchable.

Why Blogs in Addition to Something Else?

A blog provides a somewhat more formal learning space, implicitly asking for longer or reflective responses or assignments. It would therefore make a good partner with a microblogging tool like Twitter, which invites quicker, more rapid-fire interactions and may lend itself toward the quick development of community.

> **Special Consideration**
>
> More than any other tool described in this book, Blogs require writing—liking it, being good at it, or needing to practice it. This is true for both the instructor and the learners. When you can, consider using approaches that include videos, photos, or links—things that don't require so much writing. Also consider the demands on the learners' time, and weigh the value of the activity against other assignments and the payoff the assignment will provide to the learning experience. Sometimes it helps to be clear with learners the degree of "perfection" you expect: For instance, for many assignments you may just say, "Spend ten minutes on this" or "Quickly brainstorm some comments."
>
> *A trick:* Ask learners to compose as if they were writing an email to someone. They are used to this, and it may be a more realistic approximation of actual workplace performance.

Getting Started

Types of Blog Hosting Plans

Most of the blogs you've seen are likely developer-hosted blogs, like Blogger or WordPress (look in the URL of your favorite blogs to see who hosts them). They offer basic blog setup and hosting for free, with optional additional paid enhancements. If you want more customizability or control, you can opt for a third-party-hosted blog, but this requires a hosting plan and installation on a server. Your company's own IT office can also set up a blog inside the company firewall, and tools like SharePoint and Traction Software have blog-type capabilities as well.

Setting Up an Account

Go to any free blog site such as www.blogger.com or www.wordpress.com. Instructions there will provide easy directions for setting up a blog and picking a template. You might want to look around at some blogs and see what you think will best suit your needs.

Google analytics is a free tool you can use to track your websites or your blog. It will give you details about the number of times someone accesses a page, time of day, the number of times a link you posted was followed, and that sort of thing. See www.google.com/analytics.

Setting Permissions

The blog setup process will ask you to determine who can access your blog, for instance, whether it is available to the public or whether your learners must be invited or approved to view and comment. You may also choose to have comments unmoderated—anything learners post goes immediately to the blog—or whether you would prefer to approve comments first. You can also enable an email notification that will alert you any time someone comments.

Add-Ons

There are dozens of free add-ons useful for a class blog. Many are available directly from the developer (such as WordPress or Blogger) or available via the web. Most will appear on the blog in the sidebar or as a clickable button. Popular add-ons for class blogs available outside the developer blogs include, for example, Google calendar (Figure 4.3), which allows you to provide a class schedule, reminders about readings, and notices of upcoming events; digital drop boxes, which provide a way to share files (see box.net or getdropbox.com), or polling tools such as those available from www.polldaddy.com. Try a Google search for "blog widgets" to see the tools available.

You Decide

You need to make a choice as to whether you will host a single class blog, or whether each learner will be expected to set up his or her own blog. Read over this chapter and consider the ways in which you are likely to use a blog and what sorts of activities you will want to use with your learners. Asking others to set up and maintain a blog requires a good deal of commitment and work from them. Consider the relative worth of the effort required for the blog against the objectives of the course.

Figure 4.3. Google Calendar Is a Widget, Easily Added to a Blog

To be successful at using blogs in training, you, as the instructor, will need to set the example. You'll need to be consistent about using the blog and ensure that fresh content is loaded regularly so that people don't lose interest. You'll need to set the tone (conversational/informal? businesslike? stiff?), post new material, and interact with others by responding to their comments and facilitating conversation.

To Provide a Course Site or Host an Online Course

A blog can be used to host a course site (such as "23 Things" described early in this chapter or the "2012 Leadership Academy Class") or to provide ongoing support for a particular course topic (Customer Service at Acme). As a course-hosting tool you can use the blog to post weekly assignments or readings, links to videos or articles, or links to "lessons" placed on YouTube or in PowerPoint shows.

For anything you post, you can ask for learner reactions, reflections, arguments, or counter-ideas. Learners can then comment to you or to each other. You may further invite reactions, reflections, or ideas for applying concepts to the work setting.

Case: Public Library Uses a Blog to Host a Course

Helene Blowers, then technology director for the Public Library of Mecklenburg County (PLCMC), North Carolina, saw that staff technology skills were not keeping pace with the needs of library patrons and the evolving nature of library services. She developed the "23 Things" blog (see Figures 4.1 and 4.2 at the beginning of this chapter) to "encourage staff to experiment and learn about the new and emerging technologies that are reshaping the context of information on the Internet today." Stated objectives are to:

- Encourage exploration of Web 2.0 and new technologies by PLCMC staff.

- Provide staff with new tools (that are freely available on the Internet) to better support PLCMC's mission: *expanding minds, empowering individuals, and enriching our community.*

- Reward staff for taking the initiative to complete twenty-three self-discovery exercises.

While the Blogger blog itself, and the tools used (such as Flickr and YouTube) were free, Blowers obtained some funding for the project. She used this to reward staff who completed all twenty-three things by a given deadline with an MP3 player. Staff completing the twenty-three things were also entered in a drawing for the grand prize, a laptop computer. Not surprisingly, the course saw a phenomenal completion rate.

Information from http://plcmcl2-about.blogspot.com used with permission of Helene Blowers.

To Support a Traditional Course

You may choose to use a course blog to supplement or extend the experience of "live" classes held in a traditional or virtual classroom.

Pre-Work

Pre-work can serve both to help participants get to know one another better as well as inform the instructor about learner interests, backgrounds, and skills; knowledge of the subject matter; and the expectations learners bring to the training experience.

"Four Pics"

As a get-to-know-you exercise prior to class, and to help learners become familiar with the blog software you're using, ask learners to search for Creative Commons images (see Key Terms in the Introduction to this book), or use their own photos, and upload four that tell something about themselves. Depending on the functionality of your blog site, you may need to ask them to submit the photos to you by email so that you can upload them. Added plus: This will give you some idea as to who your more tech-savvy learners are. Figure 4.4 shows an example.

Skills Inventory

Help develop learner readiness for learning by encouraging a realistic assessment of current skills. In a blog post, ask learners to list a few things in the comments area—perhaps up to ten—that they've accomplished and that made them feel successful. It doesn't have to be work related (it could be building a child's tree house or volunteering for a community project). Ask them to choose three things from this list that were most important to them and to write brief narrative paragraphs or outlines describing what they did. Have them identify skills they used to accomplish the task. Encourage other learners to read over one another's comments and add their thoughts on skills they feel were likely employed.

"Questions"

Invite learners to submit a question about course content, related ideas, or "I have always wondered" in advance of starting a new topic. This will help to give you a place to focus and make the content more meaningful to the learners.

**Figure 4.4. Example of Blog-Based
"Four Pics" Activity**

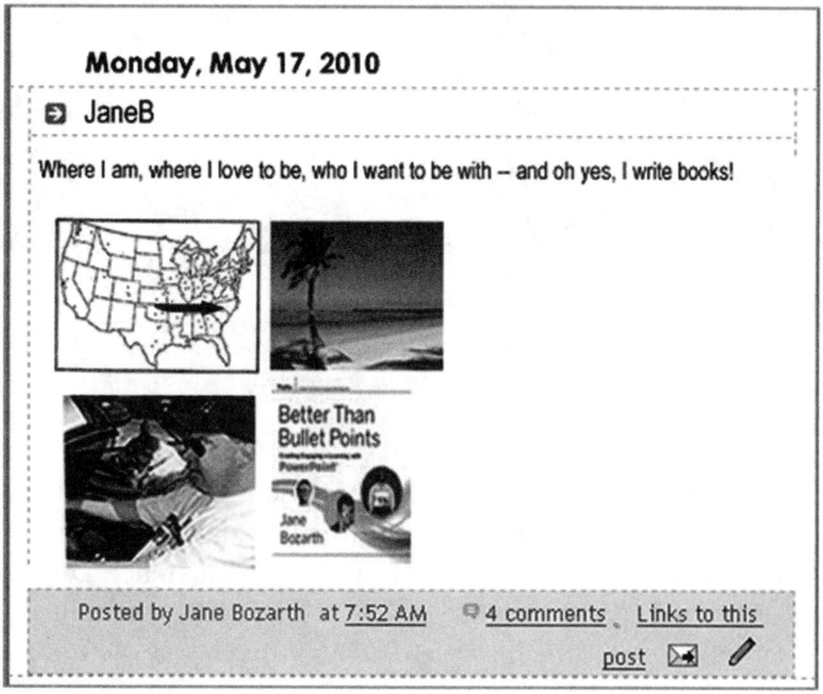

Monday, May 17, 2010

JaneB

Where I am, where I love to be, who I want to be with -- and oh yes, I write books!

Better Than
Bullet Points

Jane
Bozarth

Posted by Jane Bozarth at 7:52 AM   4 comments   Links to this
post

Virtual Sticky Notes

Use the free tool from www.pindax.com to create a virtual whiteboard on which learners can place virtual sticky notes. Link to this from the blog. Use this the way you might use sticky notes in a traditional class. Ask learners to post, for instance:

- One thing they already know about the topic

- One thing they hope to learn in the course

- Their one best tip for closing a sale

- Their best advice to a new hire

Virtual sticky notes can also be used for affinity exercises or categorizing ideas, as is often done with sticky notes in a traditional class. Figure 4.5

Figure 4.5. Pindax Virtual Sticky Note Tool

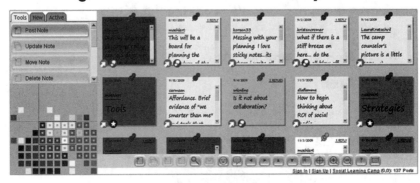

Image used with permission of Mark Oehlert, Innovation Evangelist at Defense Acquisition University (meet him on Twitter as @moehlert).

offers a view of one sticky note tool, Pindax. Mark Oehlert and his collaborators used the tool in planning for the "Social Media Bootcamp" sessions at the DevLearn 2009 conference. Different topics (or people) can be assigned different colors. The screen here shows only part of the work; the lower-left corner shows a snapshot of all the notes pinned to the virtual board.

Note: The size of the sticky note will limit responses to just a few words, making this similar to posting on Twitter. Explore Chapter 2 on Twitter for more ideas.

Intersession Work

Blogs can also provide a good online place to fill the space between formal training events.

General Discussion

Toss out any question for which everyone is likely to have an answer or opinion:

- "What ideas do you have for improving the training registration process?"

- "What are your views on accepting gifts from vendors?"

Extend discussions by responding to learner comments and asking for more:

- "Ahmed feels our current corporate culture over-emphasizes the timekeeping aspect of employment and fails to understand the real meaning of 'managing for results.' What do others think of this?"

Note: In fostering discussion and asking for responses, it's important that you provide specific context or topics to consider. For instance, not just "Reflect on your experience as a leader," but:

- "What were your expectations of being a new manager? How did they differ from the reality?

- "What transitions did you have to make when you moved from peer to supervisor?"

Figure 4.6 shows an example of a blog used for intersession work by InSync Training, LLC. The company offers several multi-session certification courses for synchronous trainers and designers, with sessions offered in the virtual classroom. Learners complete intersession assignments via the blogs moderated by course facilitators.

Hot Topics

During training, listen for hot topics (such as identifying those slated for layoffs; whether ideas about the differences in "generations" are legitimate; or what one would define as limits for accommodating a worker with a disability). Post one topic and ask learners to post a response.

- Create a post asking learners to provide a one-hundred-word recap of the critical takeaways from the past session.

- Create a post: "Yesterday we covered _____. If you had to explain the main concepts to someone else, what would you say?"

- Post a link to an article or YouTube or CNN video clip and invite learner responses.

- For a management development program, each Friday ask for a quick response to something critical that is threaded throughout the course, such as, "List five things you caught people doing right this past week."

- Provide, or ask learners to use a Google blog search to locate, three other blogs related to the course content. Ask learners to read the most recent postings on these, and respond to the post or to a comment there.

As a rule, it's a good idea for the trainer or blog facilitator to offer some prompt to which learners can respond or something akin to a "template" with an example of a sample response. This is much easier on learners than asking them to just work from a blank page. A prompt or example of a response will help facilitate and encourage learner responses.

Figure 4.6. A Blog Can Provide a Good Space for Intersession Work

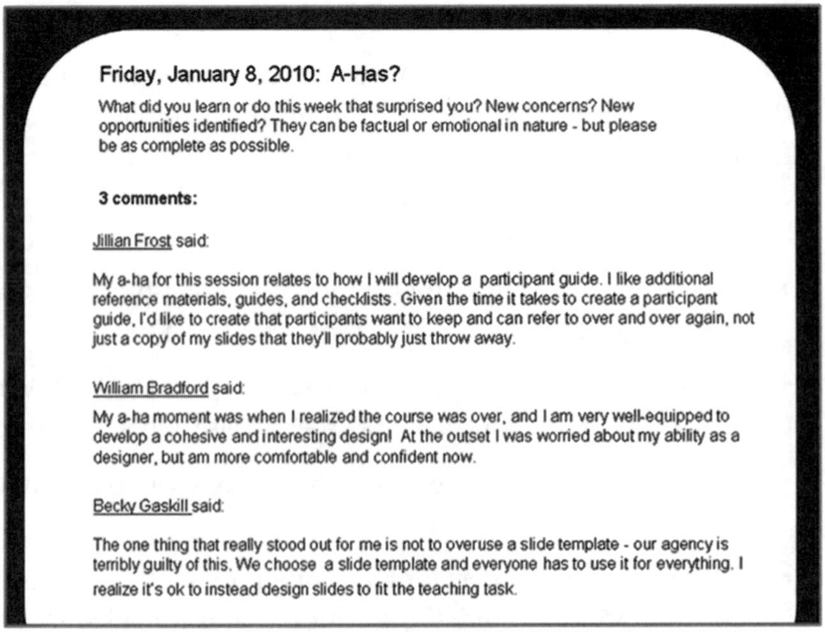

Friday, January 8, 2010: A-Has?

What did you learn or do this week that surprised you? New concerns? New opportunities identified? They can be factual or emotional in nature - but please be as complete as possible.

3 comments:

Jillian Frost said:

My a-ha for this session relates to how I will develop a participant guide. I like additional reference materials, guides, and checklists. Given the time it takes to create a participant guide, I'd like to create that participants want to keep and can refer to over and over again, not just a copy of my slides that they'll probably just throw away.

William Bradford said:

My a-ha moment was when I realized the course was over, and I am very well-equipped to develop a cohesive and interesting design! At the outset I was worried about my ability as a designer, but am more comfortable and confident now.

Becky Gaskill said:

The one thing that really stood out for me is not to overuse a slide template - our agency is terribly guilty of this. We choose a slide template and everyone has to use it for everything. I realize it's ok to instead design slides to fit the teaching task.

Scavenger Hunt

Create a blog post with links to several websites relevant to the course content. Ask learners to locate information such as "What seem to be common factors in organization social media policies?" or "How do others handle tuition reimbursement for employees?" *Important:* Choose some websites that will be of long-term use to learners—sites you would recommend they bookmark for ongoing future reference. Don't have the learners hunt down information on a site they are unlikely to use again.

Round Robin

Assign learners numbers. Create a blog post on a topic meaty enough to generate a good deal of conversation or that gives learners room to add to. Each learner posts a comment according to his or her number. For instance:

- "Tips for Good Facilitation"

- "Low-Cost Ways of Motivating Staff"

- An example of "The Customer Is Always Right"

- How can you assess whether a job candidate has been honest about his or her ability?

Figure 4.7 shows an example of a prompt for a round-robin activity. Learners are assigned numbers indicating the order in which they are to respond.

Shifting Point of View

Ask learners to write blog entries from a different angle. Have them comment as a new hire documenting her first few days at work, an insurance-claims adjuster in a town just hit by a major storm, or a customer reacting to receiving the wrong item three times.

Or choose particular course material and assign something specific to write about, preferably something that will prompt a strong opinion while demonstrating an understanding of course material, such as: "You cannot motivate performance. All motivation is internal."

Figure 4.7. "Round Robin" Blog-Based Activity

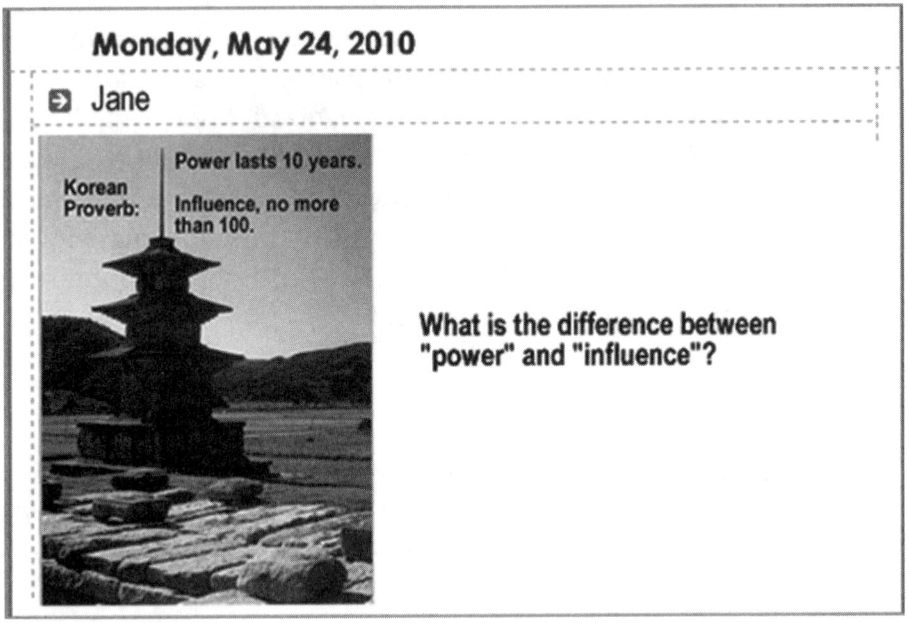

Concept Center

Create a blog-based concept center based on an idea related to the course matter. For instance, in a program covering employment policies, the blog concept center could include things such as:

- Little-known facts about the Americans with Disabilities Act

- Annotated timeline of U.S. civil rights laws

- Additional links, resources, book reviews, biographies

Alternative: Gallery Walk

As an alternative to the concept center, ask learners (rather than doing it yourself), if they have their own blogs, to create one page of the concept center. Give a deadline by which pages must be completed, then another deadline by which each learner needs to visit the other blogs.

Debate

Assign roles or positions. Provide a blog post with an overview of the question or issue, and ask learners to use the comments area to debate:

- *Bill:* "You cannot motivate performance. All motivation is internal."

- *Emmanuel:* "A good leader can elicit remarkable performance, even from those who have never exhibited it."

- *Pro and Con:* It's all right for employees to make personal calls on company time.

- *Alternative:* Learners with their own blogs may use that space to develop a fuller argument to support their "side"—with links, photos, video clips—whatever they choose to utilize.

Points of View

Identify a topic that is not contentious but can be approached from several different stances, for instance, strategies for closing a sale or ideas for approaching a particular type of project or their experience in retaining good performers. Have learners, or groups of learners, work to develop a brief online response, which could include links to other material, such as YouTube videos. This can, in turn, serve as mini-training or a presentation for others.

Case Studies

Provide a case study and invite reactions/solutions to it. This could be something as simple as an example of a completed performance evaluation, along with a transcript of the review conversation, or a complex scenario involving questions about ethical behavior. Learners can also be tasked with creating case studies. (An excellent resource on case studies is Jean Barbazette's book *Instant Case Studies*.)

Peer Helpers

Invite learners to submit a question or problem with which they have been struggling. At regular intervals post one of these and ask others to respond.

Create "Links"

Help learners connect the dots between different training activities and assignments. For instance, ask for responses to "How does the information in the Garrett article link to our class discussions of lean manufacturing?"

Culture Tour

Learners are enrolled in a training program with an emphasis on diversity (this may not be "diversity training" but could also be pertinent to, for instance, a leadership or customer service course). Assign a learner, or teams of learners, to study one culture and have them provide a blog post highlighting norms and customs important to the training group, such as attitudes toward authority figures and beliefs about the nature of working relationships.

Note that "culture" needn't always mean that of another country or ethnic group. Learners could be asked to study the "culture" of a competitor or other organization.

Virtual Field Trip

Ask each learner to visit the website of an organization similar to the one that employs the learner. (This can be broad, with learners from Yahoo asked to visit Google or MSN, or smaller, with learners from Yahoo's HR office asked to visit Yahoo's online HR office.) Instruct learners to look over items on the site, such as forums or blogs, customer service contact protocols, and mission statements. Have learners report what they found there: usefulness, the organization's attitude toward employees and clients, and ways the organization is (or is not) engaging with the community. What does the site tell about corporate culture?

For a customer service course, instruct learners (or pairs of learners) to visit three companies, stores, or online retailers/service providers and observe customer service practices. Ask each learner or team to report out via a blog post. Then ask all learners to post responses to "What are sound practices? What can we do in our own organization to copy the good things or avoid the bad?"

Reviewers of the first draft of this book had reservations about the idea of learners using a blog or other social media tool to express concerns. While I appreciate the point of view—and advise trainers not to do anything that could create repercussions for the learners—I do need to say: Concerns about organizational constraints and management practices come up in traditional training all the time. Most classroom trainers likely have a "What is said in here stays in here" rule, while knowing full well that often things do leak beyond the four walls of the classroom. If we are to give learners a full, meaningful experience, then we need to find mechanisms for providing the same opportunities that they would have in the traditional classroom. Judicious word choice, an understanding that, really, not much is "private" any more (online or elsewhere), and the goal of addressing concerns and taking responsibility for proactive behavior will help. Also, just giving thought to where discussion will be held and who will have access to it is worthwhile. A password-protected class blog, rather than having learners post their concerns on the organization's Facebook fan page, is only one way of approaching this.

Extend the discussion where appropriate. Learners sent to customer service training will often say they feel their hands are tied, that they are not empowered to give the refund, to offer a replacement product, or to bend the rule. Deeper discussion on "customer service" could include conversation about these constraints, ways to approach getting policies changed, and the leader's role in making decisions that affect the service provider's ability to resolve issues.

Interact with a Sister Community

It is not unusual in large organizations for the same training course to be offered by different trainers in different locations (or, in government, by different counties, states, or federal agencies). Identify some organizations—or another work unit in your own organization—delivering similar training programs, for instance, "Leadership Challenge" or "Crucial Conversations." Work to set up a link with the other instructor.

Learner Feedback

In a supervisory or communication-skills courses, give learners opportunities to provide written or verbal feedback. For instance, post a YouTube video (or custom video) of a performance appraisal and have learners write or, if your blog software has this feature, phone in the constructive feedback they would give to the supervisor in the video. You could, in the same way, invite feedback to the people in a work conflict, someone practicing using a defibrillator, or a health care technician interacting with a sick child. It is helpful in this exercise for learners to provide first-person actual responses, not, "Sue's tone is too harsh," but "Sue, Billy is only four, and he's scared. I know you're busy, but your tone sounded brusque and kind of harsh."

Mentoring

Ask learners to use their blogs to become the class experts on a particular topic: change management, cold calling, organizational development, employee on-boarding. They can then develop their blogs to serve as a repository of information, links, and video clips. Recommend them and their blog to other learners—or to the broader organization—as a source for mentoring/teaching others.

Alternative: Video Prompts

Many activities described in this chapter could work with a video review or video prompt. Search YouTube for keywords such as "conflict", "sales techniques" or "safety". Insert a link to the video on the class blog, then structure a discussion or debate around the video content.

Reading Reactions

Use a reading assignment to spark comment and reflection, as shown in Figure 4.8.

Support Practice

Leverage the reflective nature of the blog to ask for learner reflections as they work to implement new learning. Invite them to share their

Figure 4.8. Blog Assignment Asking for Response to Class Reading

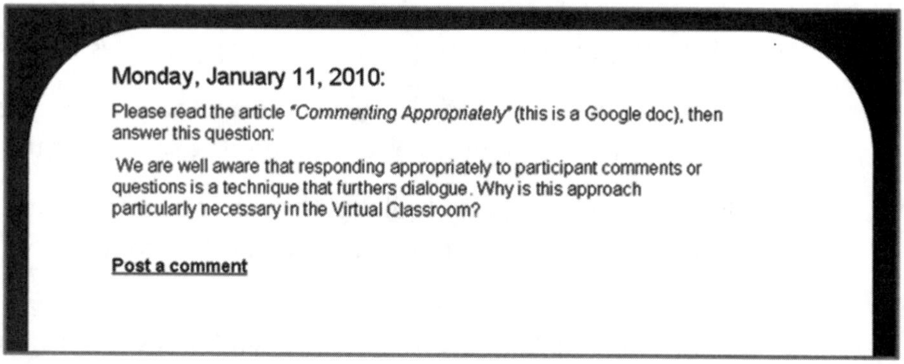

Monday, January 11, 2010:

Please read the article *"Commenting Appropriately"* (this is a Google doc), then answer this question:

We are well aware that responding appropriately to participant comments or questions is a technique that furthers dialogue. Why is this approach particularly necessary in the Virtual Classroom?

Post a comment

Like "23 Things," another perfect marriage between content and technology may have been achieved with the blog found at http://englishiwate.blogspot.com. Created by a teacher of adult learners who wishes to remain anonymous, the blog is set up as a space for Chinese students working to become English teachers to practice their English. Each student has his or her own blog and posts reflections—in English—on class activities. It is an excellent strategy for leveraging technology while providing meaningful, useful practice opportunities that are relevant to the learners' future work.

---

experiences, surprises, areas in which they felt successful, and areas in which they'd like to improve/plans for improving. Ask learners to provide coaching for one another.

Formative and Summative Evaluation

A multiple-choice or other written test only assesses short-term knowledge comprehension. If learners need to demonstrate their ability, they can prove it by posting photos or a video of themselves performing. In the "23 Things" course, for example, learners are asked to explore a new technology, then demonstrate their own use of it. Learners in a safety course might be asked to have someone video their use of proper footing when mounting a forklift, those in food service might be asked to upload a photo of a finished wedding cake, or managers could provide a sample of a memo praising recent good sales figures.

- Create a blog post asking learners to provide a one-hundred-word recap of the critical takeaways from the past session or the course.

- Use a free online survey tool such as the one at www.surveymonkey.com; create a quiz on course content and link to this from a blog post.

- Periodically ask learners to reflect on what they have learned so far. Ask them to post one test question they would ask about the content. Instruct learners to respond to each other's questions.

- Ask learners to take sixty seconds and write a one-sentence summary of the most recently covered content.

- Create a virtual "suggestion box" and ask learners to offer suggestions for tweaking content, adapting activities, or otherwise enhancing their experience.

- Link to a free online mind-mapping tool (such as www.mindmeisters.com) and have participants work together to create a recap of the course: key points, takeaways, and areas in which they feel they need further development.

Closing the Gap

Ask learners to post a response to "Think back over what we have covered in the course. How does this compare to what you knew, or believed, about the topic prior to the training? How can you incorporate your new learning into your past understanding?"

Obstacle Assessment

Many learning programs end by asking learners to develop an "action plan," which often may as well be a list of "good intentions." Rather than ask for just an action plan, invite learners to submit to you a list of barriers or obstacles they feel they may encounter as they work to implement their new learning. Have them further categorize these as "internal" ("I am uncomfortable with change") or "external" ("My boss will never go for this"). Create a blog post listing these. Invite learners to choose one or two from each category and write a specific plan for overcoming the barriers.

Final Projects

One of the advantages of Web 2.0 is that projects are not turned in for just one person (the instructor) to see. For courses requiring a final project, ask learners to post details, links, images, etc., on their blogs, then invite peer feedback. (*Advice:* Also offer some ground rules for providing peer feedback in useful, constructive ways.)

Post-Course

Once a month invite graduates to report out about implementing their new learning (you can set this up ahead of time). They can use a process they challenged, a behavior they tried, some success they experienced, or an unanticipated obstacle or outcome. If they developed an end-of-course action plan, ask them to record their progress on the blog. You can then serve as something of a performance consultant commenting on progress and coaching toward further accomplishment of goals.

If you have set up a blog as a course site, continue to post information, articles, videos, or other content to sustain the learning experience. Again, you can do this all at once and set the items to post automatically according to a schedule.

Building a Learning Community

Use a blog to deliver regular learning-related updates to former learners or even the entire organization. Most blog sites will allow you to schedule posts; you can create them all at once, then schedule them to upload at regular intervals. These could involve things like:

- Thursday morning stress tips, with comment area enabled for others to share their own

- Friday afternoon article links or book reviews

- Fun YouTube video of the week—others could contribute

Other blog content could include:

- Links to the training department calendars

- Reminders about upcoming training

- Information about offerings at local colleges

- Invitations to free webinars or other events

- Profiles of an instructor, course, or learners who have completed particular programs

- How-to posts from the training department or other learners

- Reports of current events of interest to the organization, such as news regarding ethics or safety violations

- Blog posts from a conference or other training event

- Responses to a competitor's blog posts

Most organizations have some amateur writers on staff. Invite former learners to be reporters from the field in helping you develop and post blog content. (*Advice:* Again, you will likely get better responses by suggesting a topic rather than just asking: "Could you please write something for the blog?")

Wellness Blog

Encourage employees to post ideas, links to sites or articles, and so forth, for healthy eating and exercise. Information could include tips for general wellness, such as stress management, or notes from staff regarding healthy food choices in the company cafeteria or local lunchtime eating establishments.

Work/Life Balance Blog

Use a blog for disseminating—and asking employees to add to— data important to the whole person. This could include tips for balancing

> Consider asking an expert in the field to write a guest blog. People often are willing to provide something short. If your organization ever sponsors outside speakers on specific topics, make a guest blog post part of their contract.

work and personal time for parents of young children, links to community resources for eldercare, or investment strategies and retirement planning. Other material could be ideas for staying organized and simple stress-reducing exercises. This acknowledges that the employee is more than just a worker, acknowledges life issues with which he or she is challenged, and helps to build a sense of community among those facing similar issues.

Lifelong Learning Blog

Host a blog that supports lifelong learning:

- Post information about upcoming events offered by the training department, via other avenues online, or in the community.

- Provide course updates, follow-ups, and new information.

- Enlist management's help in requiring employees attending conferences at company expense to post reflections during, or once home from, the event.

- Showcase local or distance college or graduate programs that may be of interest to employees.

- Link to reviews of tools like "iPhone apps for learners."

- Provide links to "how to" sites and videos.

- Offer showcases of interesting new technologies or ideas in fields relevant to staff.

- Provide links to free webinars, podcasts, or other easy-access learning programs.

Summary

Remember that blogs give you a very easy, simple web page. If you could create a course website, what would it look like? Odds are you'd include links, photos, video clips, articles, and perhaps PowerPoint-based lessons. You'd probably want simple discussion features and maybe a calendar or advanced search tool. Blogs can do all that, as well as provide a private (if you choose that) communication space to share with your learners.

Somewhat more formal than other Web 2.0 technologies, but good at lending themselves toward hosting a course or longer assignments, the instructor willing to look at non-traditional methods for building community will find blogs an excellent tool to replace or supplement more traditional approaches to training.

CHAPTER 5

Wikis

In a Nutshell

A wiki is an interactive web page on which everyone with access can change the content.

In a Larger Container

Wikis provide an easy-to use, editable, online space for collaborative work, sharing knowledge, and building databases or libraries of information. www.wikipedia.org is the most famous example of a wiki. Content is typically text-based, but most wiki products allow simple uploading of photos and multimedia objects.

How to View Wikis

Think of the wiki as most useful for collaboration, editorship, and data compilation. In employing wikis in training, results might include (1) learner-built development of a permanent, takeaway record of the particular course session; (2) a record of the course over various iterations or offerings across time; (3) a compilation of FAQs or good practices for those coming into the role that the training targets; (4) or a single project aimed at improving overall company or work-unit operations.

Advantages/Disadvantages of Wikis in Training

Advantages

Wikis are easy to use and learn, and everyone with permission can edit them. The software records every change made and draft created, and most wikis can be set up to alert the owner(s) when changes are made. They are excellent for collaborative work and a wonderful tool for supporting learners who are geographically dispersed. Wikis can be password-protected; the owner and other named administrators can approve users and set access levels (view or edit) for individuals. One of the early reviewers for this book, trainer Tracey Connolly from Delaware state government, said, "More than any of the other products we've looked at, a wiki taps into synergy: It's not just the trainer who is responsible for creating the final product. It also creates a shared responsibility. If something is missing or incorrect, it's not just the trainer who must find and correct it." Most basic wiki products are free, with additional space and features available at some cost. Wiki software can, also at cost, be installed inside the company firewall. Some products, like Microsoft SharePoint, include wiki functionality.

Disadvantages

Well . . . everyone with permission can edit it. Wikis, particularly as they grow, can become disorganized; approaching the class wiki or planned projects with some ideas on organizing and maintaining them will help. Anecdotal reports hold that employees are sometimes hesitant to edit one another's work, so the instructor may have to guide and facilitate this.

Why Wikis Instead of Something Else?

Whereas the other technologies discussed in this book provide a topic-response format, wikis are truly collaborative. The instructor wishing to use Web 2.0 tools for a large group project or start of a library or knowledge database would likely be happiest with a wiki.

Why Wikis in Addition to Something Else?

Again, a wiki is meant for collaborative work. Unless you choose a wiki with a dedicated discussion area (such as that provided by Wikispaces), it is not really well-suited to discussions. Because of the editing capability, there's a risk of learners engaging in a game of endless comment-delete comment-replace comment interactions. You may want both a space for collaborative work as well as providing opportunities for discussion, sharing photos, and less structured interactions. In that case, you might want to use both Facebook and a wiki. Or you may have a course focused on a large collaborative project, but want some way for learners to post quick responses to ongoing course issues and in-class discussions. So perhaps a wiki supplemented with Twitter interactions would work for you.

Getting Started

There are dozens of free wiki sites; arguably the most popular are www.wikispaces.com and www.pbworks.com. (The "pb" in PBWorks references "peanut butter" as in, "Easy as making a peanut butter sandwich.") Some sites include advertising, some limit number of users, some don't yet accommodate access from mobile phones. Google "free wiki" and look around to see what meets your needs.

Setting Up an Account

Most wiki sites will require you to have a valid email address for setting up an account. Once in, you'll be walked through the setup process. (*Advice:* If the product makes setup complicated or confusing, take that as a warning and try another product. You don't want something that will be hard for your learners, too.)

Setting Permissions and Notifications

Again, the product will walk you through the permissions process. Because you are presumably using this for collaborative work, then you'll need to give your learners editing (rather than just viewing) rights. You will probably also want to be notified by email when additions or other changes are made.

Hosting an Online Course

College instructors report success at using wikis to host an entire online course. Due to the text-heavy nature of the wiki, this appears to have been most successful with academic courses that require writing, such as

English composition. Similarly, workplace training practitioners will want to match the technology to the instructional intent. A wiki might be a good choice with, for instance, hosting a business writing, policy development, or project management course. Or, with the addition of tools for capturing audio and perhaps video, a wiki could make a nice foundation for an online foreign language program.

Case: Jive Software Uses Wiki to Host a Course

Here's an example of a wiki Jive Software uses to host a training program within its Jivespace developer community. The home page of the "Jive SBS 4.0 Developer Training Course" shows that the course has seven course topics. Let's take a closer look at Topic 6: Widgets, shown in Figure 5.1.

Figure 5.1. Choosing "6. Widgets" Takes the Learner to the Home Page for That Module

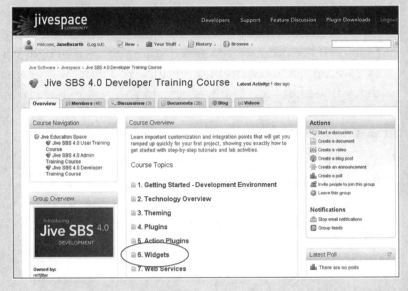

Figure 5.2. Home Page for "6. Widgets"

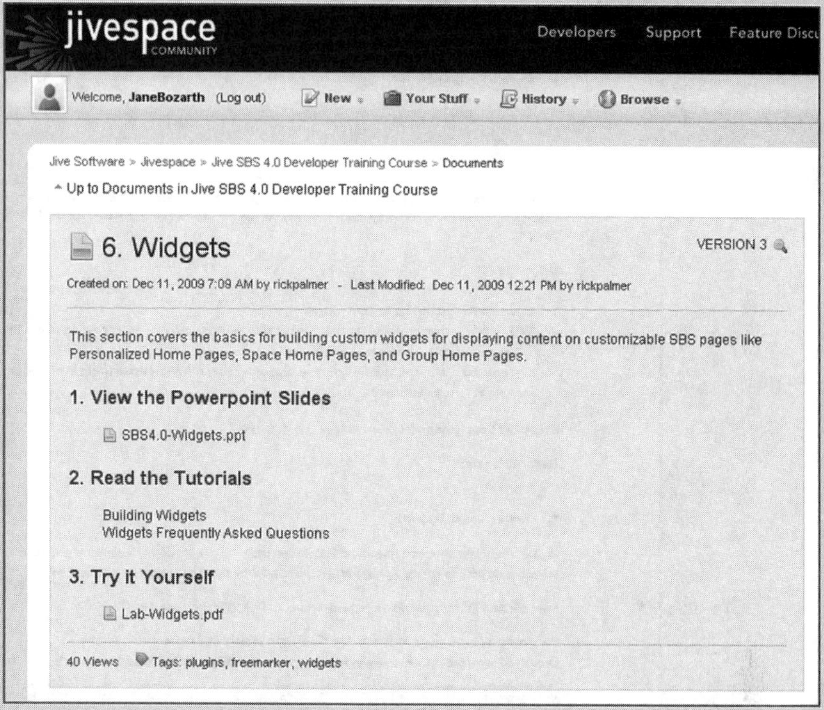

From the module home page (Figure 5.2) learners can choose what content to access. Item 1 is "View the PowerPoint slides." A sample slide is shown in Figure 5.3.

As shown in Figure 5.4, learners then choose the "Read the Tutorials" link, which takes them to the product documentation help pages.

Finally, as shown in Figure 5.5, the "Try It Yourself" link gives the learner access to a pdf-based lab exercise with detailed instructions for building a widget.

(Continued)

Figure 5.3. Screen from PowerPoint Overview of Module

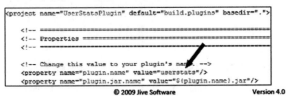

LAB: Widgets

Overview

In this lab you will create a custom widget that displays the newest users in the system. Your widget will also include a design-time property to control the number of recent user names to display.

Objectives:

1. Learn how to build a custom widget.
2. Learn how to apply different css styles to your widget's display, depending on where the widget is positioned on the screen.
3. Learn how to implement design-time properties that will allow users to customize your widget to suit their needs.

Estimated time to complete: 30 minutes

Instructions:

1. **Create a Plugin Project**

Create a new Java project named UserStatsPlugin (refer to the previous Plugin lab if you need a refresher on how to create a plugin project) and add the jive_sbs project as a dependency.

Note: Be sure that the plugin project resides in C:\Jive4.0\Project\UserStatsPlugin.

Copy build.xml and plugin.xml from the TestPlugin project and paste them into the UserStatsPlugin project. Set the plugin.name property value in build.xml to "userstats":

```
<project name="UserStatsPlugin" default="build.plugins" basedir=".">

    <!-- =====================================================================
    <!-- Properties =========================================================
    <!-- -----------------------------------------------------------------

    <!-- Change this value to your plugin's name. -->
    <property name="plugin.name" value="userstats"/>
    <property name="plugin.jar.name" value="${plugin.name}.jar"/>
```

© 2009 Jive Software   Version 4.0

Page 1

Each component of the module offers a space for learner comments, which often take the form of learners helping one another. Figure 5.6 shows this.

Figure 5.4. "Read the Tutorials" Section

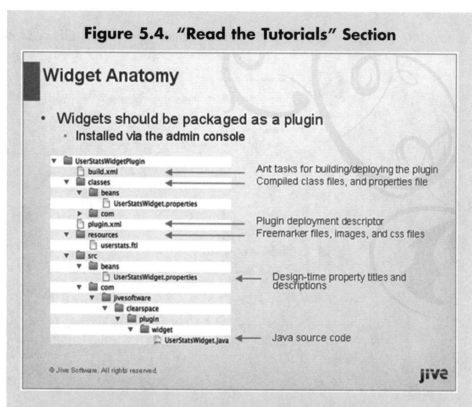

Figure 5.5. "Try It Yourself" Lab Exercise

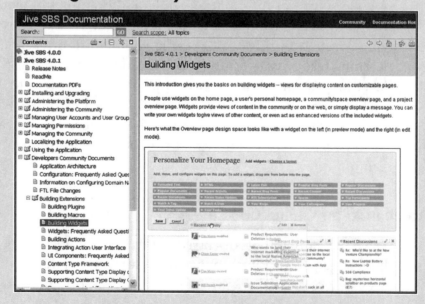

(Continued)

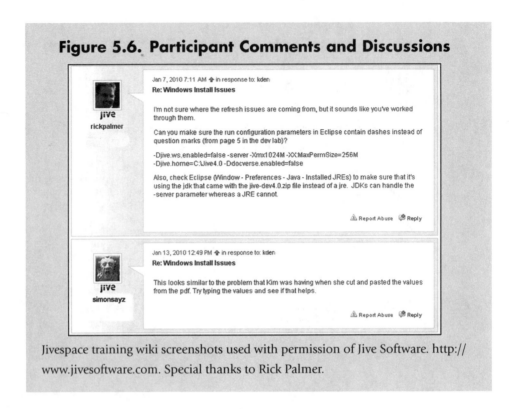

Figure 5.6. Participant Comments and Discussions

Jivespace training wiki screenshots used with permission of Jive Software. http://
www.jivesoftware.com. Special thanks to Rick Palmer.

A good source of information about and examples of using Wikis
in learning can be found at www.wikversity.org. Wikiversity (http://
en.wikiversity.org) is "a Wikimedia Foundation project devoted to
learning resources, learning projects, and research for use in all
levels, types, and styles of education from pre-school to university,
including professional training and informal learning. We
invite teachers, students, and researchers to join us in creating
open educational resources and collaborative learning
communities."

In Addition to an Online Course

As with the other tools discussed in this book, trainers using a course
built largely from asynchronous modules will find that a wiki can
provide a collaborative, engaging space to support online instruction.

Like blogs, however, wikis are somewhat more limited in their ability to support fostering a "community"; there is less personal space than with, say, Facebook. Unlike blogs, wikis are not generally thought of as an optimum space for hosting discussions. Consider the right tool for the job: If the instructional plan for the online course includes substantial collaborative work, then a wiki might be the right choice, either alone or in addition to another tool.

To Support a Traditional Course

Wikis can serve to fill in spaces between formal classroom events, helping to keep the learning experience on the "front burner" and providing a place for learners to engage with one another.

Figure 5.7 shows an example of a Wikispaces wiki set up to support a traditional course. Learners meet "live" each week and then visit the wiki to create their own recaps, access additional information, and participate in assignments. The course is an "Administrative Support Specialist" curriculum; weekly topics are listed at left.

Editing the wiki is as simple as clicking "edit," making changes on the screen, then clicking "save," as shown in Figure 5.8.

Figure 5.7. Wiki-Supported Course for Administrative Support Specialist Program

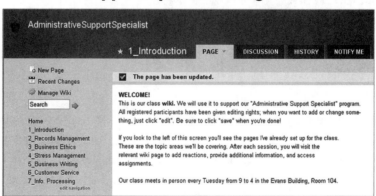

Figure 5.8. To Edit Most Wikis, Click "Edit" and "Save"

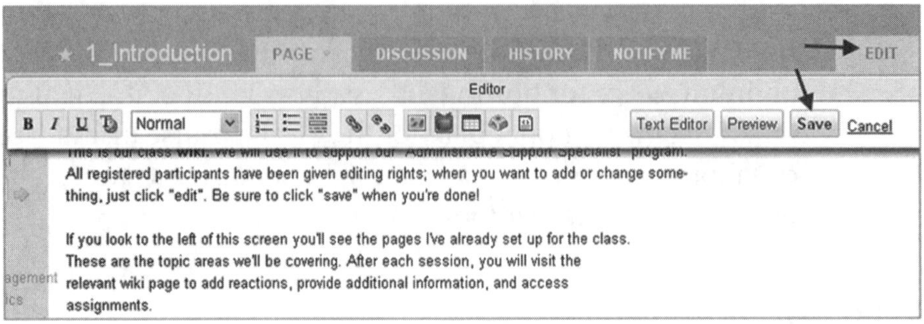

Pre-Work

Introductions

Dedicate a wiki page—or give a page to each learner—for get-to-know-you information and to set the stage for the collaborative work to come. Ask learners to reveal something about themselves, such as hobbies, favorite books, or links to favorite websites; ask for learner reasons for enrolling in the program, one thing they hope to take away, or something they already know about the topic or provide some links to articles or other information that will help set the stage for learning.

Intersession Work

As with the other tools we've seen thus far, a wiki can be a good space for working in the spaces between formal course meetings.

Projects

Learners enrolled in a train-the-trainer program are responsible for working collaboratively in developing three new interactive, engaging lesson plans on assigned topics. In a Leadership Academy exercise, learners are divided into seven groups. Each group is assigned to one of the seven criteria for the Baldridge Award. The groups then conduct an

Oxfam International works toward building lasting change in overcoming world poverty and hunger. With three thousand partners in one hundred countries, providing training to workers is a challenge—one the organization meets by delivering much training online synchronously using virtual classroom software. Oxfam International is using a wiki, along with other tools, to help learners remain engaged, continue learning, and stay connected in the intervals between scheduled training sessions.

Thanks to Cynan Houghton.

assessment of where their organization currently stands and identifies ways to improve in each area.

Have learners create a map or flow chart of a current company process, then work together to create a new, better process.

Class Notes

Wikis can help learners develop a permanent, searchable record of notes from live class sessions. Start a new wiki page for every class session and have learners create and edit notes as they go. Figure 5.9 shows a learner's recap of the "customer service" session. Different learners can enter data in different fonts, colors, or sign off with initials or simply add anonymously to the ongoing list.

Lifelines

This activity, geared toward learners who have been with the organization for a period of time, helps them become more mindful of their own learning and the long-term changes within the organization. Ask learners to create a "lifeline" beginning with their first day on the job. (This can be done with bullet points or, for more artistic learners, a drawing photographed with a digital camera, with the photo then uploaded to the wiki.) Learners should identify moments during their time in the organization when major changes occurred, critical

Figure 5.9. Wiki Page Showing Partial Learner Recap of "Customer Service" Session

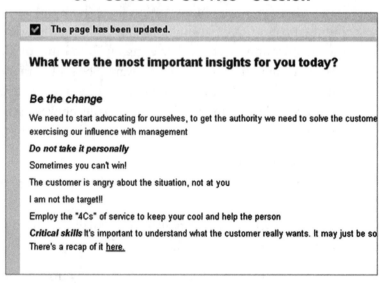

> ☑ **The page has been updated.**
>
> **What were the most important insights for you today?**
>
> *Be the change*
> We need to start advocating for ourselves, to get the authority we need to solve the custome
> exercising our influence with management
> *Do not take it personally*
> Sometimes you can't win!
> The customer is angry about the situation, not at you
> I am not the target!!
> Employ the "4Cs" of service to keep your cool and help the person
> *Critical skills* It's important to understand what the customer really wants. It may just be so
> There's a recap of it here.

incidents took place, and points the learner recalls as critical learning moments. Ask them to elaborate on each with a few key words or an image. Once learners have all uploaded their lifelines, encourage the group to work together to examine the differences in their perspectives and construct a shared understanding of the organization's history.

Reviews

Provide a wiki space for learners to post reviews of material related to the course, such as articles, blogs, books, mainstream films, other courses, or websites.

FAQs

Set up a page or pages according to topics, and ask learners to work together to build a list of frequently asked questions about topic areas. This can be set as an assignment with a time limit or continue throughout the course. This can be a takeaway for learners in a particular course or be kept as an evolving tool for all learners over multiple sessions of the same course.

Full Process

It's not unusual for employees of an organization to understand only the work of their own units. They may never see the next step in a process or the final product once it's in a customer's hands. Use a wiki with separate sections set up for workers from different areas. Invite them to create an overview of what they do using text, images, or video captured with a phone or flip camera.

Problems Solved

For classes involving discussions of organizational issues, worked problems or cases, set up a "solutions" wiki area. Ask for volunteers to document the basic issues and solutions generated by the group.

Advice Pages

Ask learners to contribute to the creation of advice pages for future learners or for others in the organization in similar job roles or having similar tasks. Advice pages might include just that—advice from more seasoned learners to the more novice—as well as lists of useful links, suggestions for useful YouTube videos, or annotated reading lists. (*Note:* Organizations interested in peer mentoring might find this a good place to start.)

"Dear Wiki" Letter

This is a twist on the case study: Learners are asked to work together and create a response to a "Dear Wiki" letter. Assign learners to groups of three to five people each. Create a wiki page for each group and post a "letter to Wiki" there. Instruct groups to work together to create a response. Your letter should include an introduction, provide some background/context, present a problem or decision, and a request for advice. See the following sample letter.

Dear Wiki,*

I am writing for advice on how to implement performance-improvement measures at my company. A few weeks ago I became an overwhelmed new hire at a corporate training vendor. My new employer is a small company that develops and delivers customized technology training to corporate customers. We also deliver a variety of computer-skills training courses (PowerPoint, Excel, Word) from our catalog. All of the training is classroom-based and I lead the training design team.

There are a growing number of customer complaints about staff turnover. A project starts with one rep and closes with another who is not adequately informed. Clients no longer feel secure when a different rep approaches them each time without knowing the background of the company's relationship. What should I do?

---

*"Dear Wiki" material adapted from Watkins, R. (2005) *75 e-learning activities*. San Francisco: Pfeiffer. This material is reproduced with permission of Pfeiffer, an imprint of John Wiley & Sons, Inc.

Reflection

One strategy I have used throughout my career, whatever I was teaching, is a little exercise taken years ago from training materials originally developed by Development Dimensions International (DDI) for their Interaction Management course. Following the demonstration of a skill, a skill practice or role play, or teach-back of a skill, learners must answer the following questions:

- "What was the best thing I did?"

- "If I did this again tomorrow, what would I do differently?"

Note that the second question is *not* "Would I do anything differently?" (a closed-ended, yes-no question) but "What would I do" differently (an open-ended question requiring an answer, implying that there is always room for improvement, a change, or trying something differently.) Used consistently, this builds the habit of reflective practice and sets the stage for practice back on the job. Learners need to give themselves feedback, as feedback from others may not always be available.

Once people have posted their answers on the wiki, others may contribute additional feedback.

Jigsaw

The jigsaw technique asks learners, or groups of learners, to each take responsibility for a different "piece" of learning. For instance, for learners enrolled in a team-building course, set up a wiki and assign learners to sections such as types of teams, stages of team development, team goals, conflict management, and team roles. Each group is responsible for becoming knowledgeable in, and providing a useful wiki page on, their section.

Virtual Poster

A virtual poster is a good way to present a lot of content about a topic area and will likely be more interesting than a lecture or bulleted PowerPoint show. Ask learners, or groups of learners, to create posters of information useful to their peers. These can include quotes, images, links, audio clips – whatever learners want to use.

For example, learners in a course for community service providers might create posters on aging and community services available for eldercare, child nutrition support services, and medical services available through the public health department. (*Note:* These would be useful as public documents, too, to be shared outside of the confines of the class.)

E-Portfolios

Work with learners in a job skills or career center program to develop their online e-portfolios. Assign a page to each learner and help him or her develop sections relevant to his or her career: photos of finished work, writing samples, presentations, sales or other figures showing results, peer feedback, or a demonstration of networking skills. Invite learners to help peer review and edit each other's portfolios.

Learner-Created Cases

Assign learners to groups and create a wiki page for each group. Ask learners to pool their knowledge and experience to craft a short case related to course content, for example, an instance of possible sexual harassment. Groups then access the next group's case and provide responses. (For instance, Group 1 responds to Group 2, Group 2 to Group 3, and Group 3 back to Group 1.) The case should be short, but complete enough so that others can answer: "Is this harassment? Why or why not?" "What guidelines apply in this case?" "What impact does this have on the workplace?" "If you were the 'victim,' what would you do?" "Which element of the case is most damaging?" and "What would you do?"

For instance: "John was head of a military EEO office. He frequently said things to one of the female staff members like, "OK, babe?" and "Listen here, woman." He would yell at her for leaving the office and would sometimes try to prevent her from leaving by blocking the doorway. John once complained to another manager that he had "dumb females" working for him.**

Class Book

Use a wiki as the basis of a takeaway class book. Include sections for presentation notes, copies of handouts, copies of presentations, and artifacts or documents developed during the course. Have learners develop a section on resources: websites, blogs, and/or books they found useful or would recommend as future reference. Don't forget to include a table of contents!

Post-Course

The wiki could serve as an ongoing, living tool as learners in the field work to implement new learning. Updates on and reviews of new resources found, additions to lists of FAQs, and a "lessons learned" page would help to extend the course beyond the end date.

**EEO example from Mel Silberman. (2005). *101 ways to make training active*. San Francisco: Pfeiffer. This material is reproduced with permission of Pfeiffer, an imprint of John Wiley & Sons, Inc.

Formative and Summative Evaluation

Assuming the wiki is being used to support collaborative work, the projects should be revealed as the class unfolds (formative evaluation) and upon its conclusion (summative evaluation). Other activities will give you additional information. For instance, reading over the learners' recaps of session notes will let you see whether the course is meeting their needs and your instructional goals, and activities like "Dear Wiki" will give insight into whether the learners are synthesizing and thus able to apply new learning.

Building a Learning Community

Wikis are exceptional tools for supporting knowledge sharing. Used as an organizational tool, rather than just something associated with a particular training course, a wiki can serve as an excellent vehicle for knowledge management, a way of capturing lessons learned, and helping people "connect the dots" between an organization's work units and functions.

Famous examples of successful organizational wikis are those used by Intel (Google "Intelepedia"), Pzifer, IBM, and Element K. The wikis consist of things like lists of acronyms and abbreviations, general knowledge centers, suggestions for readings and lists of links, product information useful to the sales force, team initiative updates (especially useful for those who move among several project teams), lists of available projects, overviews of who's working on what, FAQs, and solutions found.

Wikis are also popular tools for practitioners in a particular community, rather than employed by a single organization. For instance, the "Library Success" Best Practices wiki collects contributions from librarians

> In making decisions about using social media, give thought not just to the tool, but to the approach: What will help your learners talk to one another? What will help them learn?

worldwide. Now several years old, it has grown to dozens of pages on topics ranging from materials selection and services for special groups to strategies for marketing your library's services and library management and leadership. Used by the training department, a wiki can be an excellent tool for keeping training manuals and materials up-to-date.

Summary

The trainer making effective use of wikis will find them an excellent platform for projects and other collaborative work and a vehicle for creating a record of the course over one offering or through various iterations. It can also be used to create a record and compilation of takeaways for the learners.

As with the other tools covered in this book, successful integration of wikis into training programs requires a good deal of thought and planning. Outlining what you want to accomplish and drafting a general idea of how the wiki will be structured will help your learners make sense of it. Helping learners become comfortable with the product, especially with the concept of adding to or changing the work of others, will be critical to success in using the tool.

Other Tools

In this chapter I present an overview of other popular or emerging tools that can serve as add-ons to the tools discussed in Chapters 2 through 5. New products are launched and change all the time, so keep your eyes open for new and evolving tools.

Google Wave (www.wave.google.com)

Google Wave was unveiled in late 2009 and is still in the tweaking phase. It's something of a cross between email and a wiki with threaded discussion, with Wave participants able to jump in and out of the conversations and scroll backward and forward through the content of a wave. Moderators have some control over who can join a wave and who can add to or edit comments. Figure 6.1 shows an example of a wave. Wave comments can incorporate images and video, as shown in Figure 6.2.

Google Wave is adding new features all the time, including additional options for users. For example, if you begin a wave, you can set permissions for your users and limit how they can participate or whether they can edit one another's comments.

Wave extensions are also being added all the time. These extensions, much like widgets for blogs, provide additional functionality to a wave. Early extensions to Google Wave include video chat, conference calling, and Google maps.

Figure 6.1. A "Wave" in Google Wave

Wave was originally offered only in limited release, but is now available to anyone. Wave provides a shared communication space, so most activities described in this book would be workable using Wave.

Google Docs (www.docs.google.com)

Google Docs allows you to upload any file—such as a text document, spreadsheet, or presentation—and share it with others for viewing or editing. (You choose who has viewing or editing rights.) Stored files do not have to be downloaded: You—and others, if you like—can work with them as online materials together, in real time. Whole folders may be uploaded as well. Users with access can quickly share, analyze, and edit information. Google Docs also allows users to view changes

Figure 6.2. Video Incorporated into a Wave

An aside: Google Docs has another benefit for trainers. I travel a good deal so store my session PowerPoint programs, handouts, and other materials in Google Docs. Then when I travel, I can just access them anywhere I have an Internet connection. This has saved me several times, including once when an external USB drive failed, and another when I caught an error in a handout after arriving onsite to deliver the program.

and roll back to earlier versions of documents. Completed files can be published to sites like blogs and web pages. Figure 6.3 shows my view of Google Docs. Google Docs also offers an easy-to-use forms tool. Forms can double as course surveys., evaluation forms, or quizzes, as shown in Figure 6.4.

YouTube (www.youtube.com)

YouTube is a free vehicle for storing and distributing videos. Trainers can set up free accounts; an account gives the account owner a "channel" to

Figure 6.3. Google Docs User Home Page

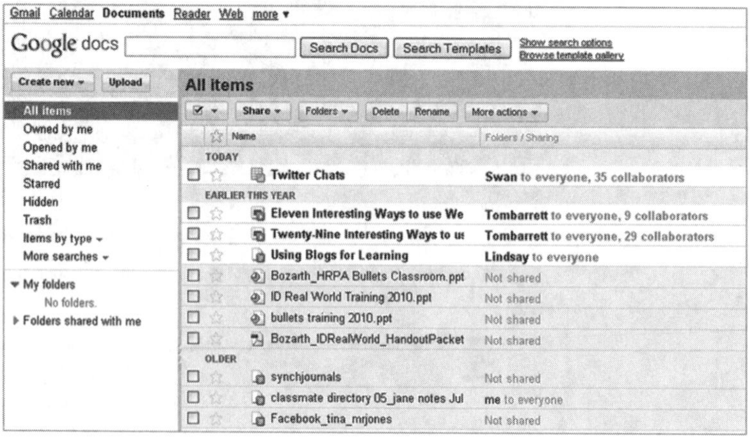

Figure 6.4. Google Docs Form Creator

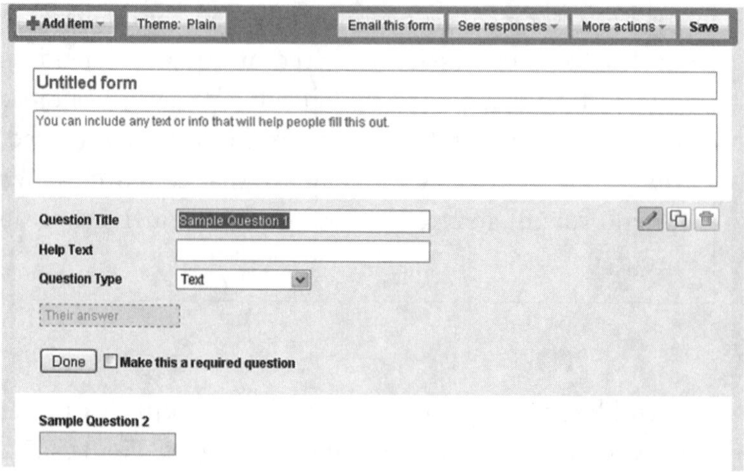

which he or she can upload material. Learners can then subscribe to the channel. The trainer can set viewing permissions, allowing access only to subscribers or to any YouTube user.

YouTube generates a piece of HTML code for each video, giving viewers a link for embedding it on an external site, for instance, a blog or web page, or adding it as a link to a Facebook or Twitter post.

On the YouTube site, videos are displayed with space for text comments or video responses. Trainers wishing to use YouTube as a standalone product (that is, without linking to videos from within another site) can use the comment area for learner reactions and trainer-learner discussion.

As the trainer, you may direct learners to view videos anywhere on YouTube, or you may choose to upload your own. I use YouTube to

Case: Interactivity via YouTube

Online personality TonyaTko recognizes the potential of YouTube and uses it very effectively to engage with her audience. Figure 6.5 shows an example of one strategy, inspired by a video that TonyaTko originally did in 2009. The trainer is discussing personal risk taking and realizing goals and asks, "What would you do if you knew you could not fail? Type your answer in the comments area." The trainer then simply stops talking—with the camera still running—and stands quietly for half a minute or so, camera running, to give viewers time to respond. She then concludes with some comments on moving forward and achieving goals. In this instance, viewers "interact" with the speaker, and the viewer comments created a wonderfully poignant record of everyone's dreams—and, it is hoped, some impetus to act.

Figure 6.5. YouTube as a Conversation Tool

store video clips to which my organization holds the copyright, to run
tutorials on software applications (I created these with SnagIt, a low-cost
screen capture tool from TechSmith that allows for simple recording

---

A Useful YouTube Trick

Does the relevant part of the content begin halfway through the video? You can tweak the code so that the video begins playing at the right moment. For instance, if the you want the video to begin playing 1 minute, 42 seconds in, add #t=01m42s to the end of the YouTube URL (#t=XXmYYs for XX mins and YY seconds).

So, if the YouTube URL is http://www.youtube.com/watch?v=z6h1DULGths, you would change it to http://www.youtube.com/watch?v=z6h1DULGths#t=01m42s by pasting #t=01m42s to the end. That's the link you'll provide to learners or paste into Facebook, your blog, or other site. When viewers access the clip, it will begin playing at 1:42.

---

with narration), and to direct learners to material on content covered in our e-learning programs, such as workplace violence and public speaking.

With the cost of flip cameras now at less than US $100, and with many cell phones now equipped with video cameras, learners can shoot their own video as well and upload it to share with the instructor and other learners. Video can also serve as formative assessment following training in a topic: Have learners submit video of themselves driving a forklift, conducting a practice evacuation, or dancing the tango.

YouTube Mobile

YouTube videos will play well on many cell phones; those using smartphones like iPhone, BlackBerry, and Android can download a free application that gives functionality equal to that of the full-version online site. Learners can both view videos on and upload videos to YouTube. Figures 6.6 shows YouTube search on an iPhone. Figure 6.7 shows the screen with playback controls; these

Figure 6.6. YouTube iPhone Search Results for "Safety Training"

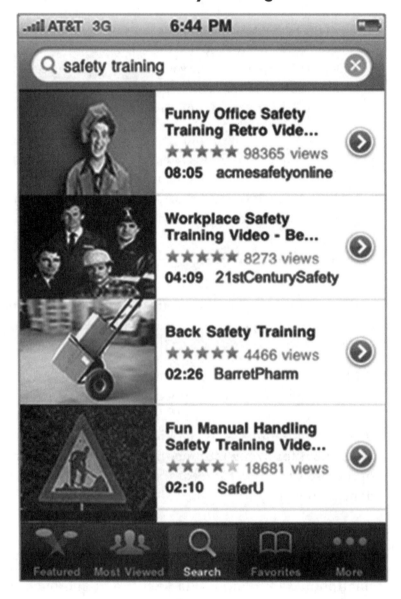

Figure 6.7. YouTube Video Running on iPhone

fade out after a few seconds but can be brought back by touching the screen.

TeacherTube (www.teachertube.com)

TeacherTube is a video sharing website similar to, and based on, YouTube. It's designed to allow those in education to share resources, and is usually considered acceptable even within organizations that block YouTube.

TeacherTube has expanded to provide capability for uploading other content as well, including audio, photos, and documents. There is also a place for blog postings and community discussion forums. Figure 6.8 shows part of the Teacher Tube home page. The TeacherTube interface looks very much like YouTube's, with space for comments below the video, as shown in Figure 6.9.

Figure 6.8. Partial TeacherTube Home Page Shows Featured Videos and Documents

Figure 6.9. TeacherTube Provides an Area for Comments

Figure 6.10. TeacherTube Interfaces with Facebook

TeacherTube interfaces well with Facebook. Those using Facebook to support or host a training program may choose to upload the a video to TeacherTube, share it on Facebook, then link viewer comments directly back to Facebook, as shown in Figure 6.10.

Social Bookmarking

Social bookmarking allows users to share, organize, search, and manage bookmarks of web resources. This is not file sharing. Only web addresses, not materials, are stored and shared. For instance, in

Figure 6.11. Example of Social Bookmarking in Delicious

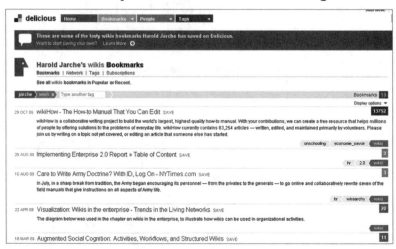

This image appears courtesy of Harold Jarche and is reproduced with permission of Yahoo! Inc. ©2010 Yahoo! Inc. Delicious and the Delicious logo are registered trademarks of Yahoo! Inc.

researching this book I was looking for examples of workplace training using wikis. I sent a note out on Twitter and within just a few minutes had a number of responses. One was from Harold Jarche (@hjarche), who sent a link to items he had bookmarked on delicious.com and tagged "wiki." Figure 6.11 shows a partial screen from this link (http://delicious.com/jarche/wikis).

Trainers can use social bookmarking to direct learners to multiple sites on a topic or structure an online scavenger hunt. Learners can identify and share bookmarks they have found on a given subject.

SlideShare (www.slideshare.net)

SlideShare offers a free place to store and share presentations. As often as not these take the form of PowerPoint shows, but SlideShare also allows for sharing documents such as PFD files. Users set up free accounts to which others can subscribe; those uploading materials can decide whether to limit viewing only to their subscribers. Links to materials are generated so that users can share them. Like Google Docs, SlideShare would be useful for trainers wishing to distribute a PowerPoint show or PDF file via Facebook, Twitter, or another social networking site.

Free Virtual Classroom Tools

Many trainers likely already have access to a web conferencing/virtual classroom tool like WebEx, Elluminate, or Adobe Connect. Those who find the cost of such products beyond their reach may want to take a look at some comparable free tools such as Dimdim (www.dimdim.com), WiZiQ (www.wiziq.com) or Tinychat (www.tinychat.com). Dimdim and WiZiQ provide functionality similar to the more commercial products, with tools such as display for PowerPoint slides, shareable online whiteboards, and text chat. Tinychat offers quick set-up video conferencing with text chat. Be aware that, as the products are free, there are often limitations as to number of participants allowed in a session or amount of moderation/control the trainer is given.

If your organization uses one of the big-name web conferencing vendors, learners with iPhones can now download free applications for accessing virtual classroom sessions and engage in live online collaborative work. As this book goes to press, both WebEx and Adobe Acrobat Connect offer apps, with more companies promising to launch their versions soon.

Skype (www.skype.com)

Skype is a service that allows users to make free voice calls worldwide via the Internet (computer-to-computer) and, for a small charge, from computers to landline and mobile phones. But that is only the beginning: Skype provides conference calling, video chat, instant messaging, searchable chat archives, and file transfer capabilities. The next iteration—now in development—promises to add simple web conferencing features like screen sharing and a virtual shareable whiteboard.

Whereas most of the activities described in this book assume asynchronous work, such as people checking into Facebook at different times of the day, Skype provides for real-time, live interaction. Applications for training are myriad. A few ideas are virtual office hours, support for foreign language instruction, reaching learners in remote locations, and bringing in subject-matter experts or authors.

Consider ways new tools can help provide a more inclusive environment for learners with different cultural, economic, or education backgrounds—or those coping with life challenges.

"We've used Skype with a second grader who is undergoing chemotherapy treatments so he can check in with his class."

Josh Allen

VoiceThread (www.voicethread.com)

VoiceThread is a web-based tool that allows for sharing an online presentation. Viewers can comment on the presentation in five ways, including phoning comments in, and can annotate the presentation (called "doodling") along with their comments. It is easy to switch identities, that is, members of a class can contribute without everyone having to have a separate login.

Mashups: Game Changers

A "mashup" is the result of a web developer literally "mashing" two technologies together. We saw an example in Chapter 2 with TweetDeck, a single product that will let you view feeds from multiple sites at once. Facebook Connect allows you to access multiple websites (such as TeacherTube) or other products (like Skype) from your Facebook account. At the time of this writing, there is a rumor of a similar Twitter Connect service in the works.

Among the most promising of the social media mashups is Posterous (http://posterous.com), which allows you to post items like posts or videos simultaneously to Twitter, Facebook, and YouTube simply by sending an email.

UStream (www.ustream.tv)

UStream is a free tool for live video broadcasting from a computer, mobile, or iPhone. Users can interact via Ustream functions to engage in activities such as rating items, taking polls, and text chatting. It is common now to see UStream users broadcasting live from iPhones with video capability.

Summary

One of the best features of the Web 2.0 tools is the ease with which one can extend them. Using a blog or Facebook, but want folks to hear one another's voices? Bring in a Skype chat. Using Facebook and want to deliver a real-time presentation? Broadcast yourself with UStream. Free, easy-to-use tools are emerging and evolving all the time to help you create your own mashups. If you can think it up, there's probably technology somewhere you can adapt to your own needs. Experiment, try to stay abreast of industry news, and be willing to learn along with your learners.

The Bigger Picture

In this book I have outlined technologies and activities to be used specifically in training activities within the purview of the individual trainer or the training department. But social media tools in business aren't really maximized by containing them in that way. Social media allows for work units, professions, colleagues, and whole organizations to better connect, share, and learn, all while spanning space and time. Helping leaders in organizations view knowledge as belonging to the collective good, rather than as proprietary pieces of data, and encouraging movement toward a culture of sharing will benefit you, your training department, and your organization.

While not explicitly described in these terms, most of the activities listed in this book are based on a belief in the value of learning in a social way: LinkedIn question-and-answer conversations, Facebook discussion forums, Ning-based book club discussions, and Twitter chats about lessons learned all, one way or another, help to support and facilitate people learning from one another, rather than just provide for expert-trainer-to-learner transmission of data. In the same way, social media supports social learning by helping people connect with one another, rather than depending on organizational top-down communication.

In this chapter we'll take a look at social learning on an organizational level and ways the organization's training function can support it.

Well First, What is "Learning"?

Clark Quinn offers perhaps the best definition of "learning": "Learning encompasses retention and transfer of new information." Regardless of how the information is gathered (for instance, from a trainer, from trial and error, from watching someone else), can the person remember the information, then make sense of it in context and apply it appropriately? The context of a problem—an opportunity to use the learning—triggers relevant associations with it, and as Quinn notes, "the more associations to information that's relevant, the more likely we are to bring useful frameworks to bear. Consequently, we are able to make connections between our understanding, knowledge, and contexts" (Quinn, 2009).

One challenge in supporting learning within an organization is that we so often don't realize when it's happening. Those who are learning don't always think of it as "learning," nor do they always think of themselves as "adult learners." More often they call it "solving a problem." An adult who wants to add a deck to his house likely doesn't say,

---

Perhaps the most stunning public example of someone "bringing useful frameworks to bear" was demonstrated on the morning of January 15, 2009, when Chesley B. "Sully" Sullenberger successfully landed a disabled jet on New York City's Hudson River. Hours and hours of practice, both in real situations and on flight simulators, had taught him a great deal about landing planes, reviewing options, and remaining calm in a crisis. There had been simulator practice in water landings. But nothing had physically taught Sully to safely land a jet on a busy river in midtown Manhattan. In confronting the problem of a disabled plane and few options for landing it, Sully had many, many associations to bring to that new context, which ultimately, cumulatively, gave him the knowledge and physical skills he needed to land the plane safely. Proof of Sully's learning over time, via acquiring new information, then retaining and transferring it, was dramatically apparent.

"I'm a motivated adult learner and I believe I'll seek out effective and engaging learning activities." She says, "I want to build a deck. How do I do it?" Or she asks a buddy, or buys a book, or Googles it, or orders a video, or signs up for a workshop at the local hardware store. Helping learners and organizational leaders recognize that "learning" is about retaining and transferring new information—not passively listening to a presentation or taking multiple-choice assessments—will help move your workforce toward becoming members of a true learning organization.

What Is Social Learning?

A good deal of learning happens via simple stimulus-response: We touch a hot stove, and we learn not to do it again. We learn by trial and error, by playing with a new piece of software or experimenting with a new recipe. But for the most part, all day long, every day, from the time we are babies, we learn from living within our culture. We learn to speak the language that is around us, sometimes with the help of explicit instruction ("Don't say 'me are going,' dear"), but more often simply by picking it up from living within it. We learn ways of dressing like others around us, rules of living in our communities, standards of social etiquette, and strategies for getting along with teachers and peers. We may memorize multiplication tables while seated at a desk, but we learn street smarts elsewhere. And as adults we do the same thing while living in the culture of our workplace, with its jargon, unspoken rules, standard operating procedures, and politics of getting along and maybe even getting ahead.

Thus, much of what we learn, we learn socially, through watching and talking with and living alongside one another. Despite what the academic model might have us believe, knowledge isn't just "transferred" from one person to another, and it isn't something we can just put into cups and pour into someone's head. But the word "social" can be tricky: It isn't just about humans interacting in some physical space. For instance, remember the person in our earlier example, the one who wanted to build a deck? She may read information on Google (that someone put there), watch a video (that someone produced), or go to a workshop (that someone is providing). And yes, she may choose to learn by trial and error, but her idea of "deck" is likely based on a cultural notion of what "deck" is, looks like, and is built of.

Another example: As I write this book, right now, alone (well, except for a certain Welsh corgi who's keeping my feet warm), I am thinking of *you*. My goal is to help you understand ways of using social media to enhance and extend your training practice. I chose activities I felt were manageable and that would be successful for you. I considered what would be useful for your learners, suggesting things that would likewise be successful for them without embarrassing them or causing discomfort. I tried to include enough information about social media products to enable you to use them without too much struggle, while not belaboring the instructions. I've encouraged you again and again to try the tools with your colleagues or your learners, as just reading about them is not enough. Learning to use them will, then, be via "social" means. (Funny thing about social media tools: You can't use them by yourself.) I may not always have it right, but every word was chosen, every section included or cut, with you, the reader, in mind. And *that* is "social."

Theory on social learning first appeared with early work from Vygotsky and was expanded a good deal in the 1970s by Albert Bandura, but it's evolved quite a bit since then. If you're especially interested in social learning in the abstract and in the workplace, try reading up on social psychology, social anthropology, and cultural anthropology.

What Does Social Learning Look Like?

While people learn formally, for instance, during a scheduled classroom event, much social learning is Informal. At its most basic level:

> In work life, socially-based learning is going on all the time in interaction between peers and across hierarchies, genders, functional groups and ages, but it often happens in modes that are not officially recognized as learning. For example, there is learning when employees discuss a new HR initiative during lunch, when Account Associates exchange customer information

in the bowling alley, when service technicians exchange war
stories at the morning coffee break, when managers linger after
a meeting to talk, or when an operator drops by a co-worker's
cubicle and notices a new screen configuration.

Brigitte Jordan,
www.lifescapes.org/Papers/0212_from_training_to_learning.htm
and used with her permission.

Social learning also happens in more structured, intentional ways—
although, again, those who are learning may not think of what they
are doing as "learning." Some well-known structures for social
learning include personal learning networks (PLNs) and communities
of practice (CoPs).

Personal Learning Networks (PLNs)

A popular term in 2010 is "personal learning networks "(PLNs). PLNs
have always existed, although we have only recently started calling them
that. Our PLNs are made up of the people we turn to when we need an
(accurate, quick) answer, when we need some help solving a problem,
when we read something interesting and want to share it with someone.
Social media tools have, for many of us, changed the nature of PLNs. In
my own case, Twitter has become my primary PLN, and my reach has
extended to colleagues as far away as New Zealand, Greenland, and
China. My contacts are primarily those associated with workplace
learning endeavors, but also elementary school teachers, college
professors, technology integration specialists, and social media experts.
But there are also librarians, a bath-oil manufacturer, world's oldest
Twitterer 104-year-old Ivy Bean, and even a few show business
celebrities who interact with me on Twitter.

I'm employed by the North Carolina state government. In my case, there
simply is no one else in my physical world—at my office, within my
agency, among co-workers, or even in North Carolina state government
involved in training—who does what I do. I really have no peers to talk
to, to throw questions to, or to learn from day-to-day. So Twitter gives
me a PLN—people I can ask, who are interested in what I'm reading,
and who can provide a "Hey, Joe!" response when I need an answer.

In your organization that reality may be very different. You may have everyone located in one building, doing similar work, who can just go talk to one another (although there is sometimes something to be said for finding perspectives beyond your day-to-day physical reach). But wherever it resides, your PLN is the place to interact socially with peers or others in a position to help you enact your work. In the space of three recent consecutive days, on Twitter, I was able to access: someone who could read Portuguese to help me decipher a permissions form from a foreign publication; a recommendation for an iPhone application that would send traffic alerts based on my location; and a citation for an article I remembered in the most vague terms someone mentioning a week earlier.

Harold Jarche, performance consultant and partner in the Internet Time Alliance, explains the importance of PLNs:

> "When it comes to the kind of work that we get paid to do, the **simple** work is being automated and the merely **complicated** work is being outsourced to where labor is cheapest. This leaves us with the **complex** work, or the type of problems that require creativity, inductive reasoning and often require help or inspiration from others.

> "Complex work and work in complex environments require faster feedback loops. We need to get data, information, and knowledge quickly and cannot wait for it to be bounced up and down a chain of command. Social networks, which are comprised of people we trust in some way, can enable us to connect to someone who may be able to help. However, to do this, we have to already have that connection. Social media allow us to initiate and nurture relationships with many people in many different ways. The quality of our networks becomes critical in enabling us to do complex work. Social learning is the enabler."

Harold Jarche
http://www.jarche.com/2009/11/the-value-of-social-media-for-learning/ Used with his permission.

People at all levels of the organization will naturally develop their own PLNs. The organization and training department seeking to help extend or support these would do well to look for ways to help employees connect with each other and find the information they need. Posting profiles of people and searchable lists of their areas of expertise and interests is a good start. Facebook groups for line staff, a wiki for the software engineers, or a blog for graduates of the in-house Six Sigma program are all ways of supporting this. Google for case studies of successful organizational wikis or other initiatives: IBM, Element K, and Pfizer—and many others—have all publicized their success with organizational wikis.

Communities of Practice (CoPs)

If we look at social learning in the workplace as occurring in layers, the first layer might be Googling and asking someone in the next cubicle. The next layer is the PLN, that network of people you trust and with whom you can interact, either face-to-face or via some other means. The next level, then, might be the community of practice (CoP), something less loosely constructed than the PLN. A community of practice includes *practitioners* engaged around some common endeavor, sharing common points of reference, with the goal of getting better at it—whether that is framed as "learning" or not.

Communities of practice are focused around *practice*—not a hobby, like stargazing, and not a community in the sense of location, like a neighborhood—but people working to improve practice and enact more skillful work. CoPs can take several forms; several examples are available to us as extended case studies.

Wenger

The seminal work on CoPs is Etienne Wenger's *Communities of Practice: Learning, Meaning, and Identity* (1998). Wenger's CoP of interest was a group of insurance claims processors. All were engaged in similar work, all in the same organization and working in the same building. Wenger took special note of the ways in which the claims processors had developed their own "repertoire" as a group—the jargon they used, the forms they did (or did not) fill out to the letter, the response to a particular type of claimant. He also noted that this sort of community—of existing workers, into which new hires were integrated—revealed a trajectory. Newcomers engaged in legitimate peripheral participation and, as they became more adept at functioning in the community, gradually moved toward expertise. As Wenger noted, it's important to note that the word "community" does not always imply harmony. As with any social structure, there are power issues and political struggles within most CoPs. (*Working Smarter: Informal Learning in the Cloud* author Jay Cross has observed that often what looks like a performance problem may be the result of exclusion from the community and its information.)

Something critical about the idea of CoPs: Wenger introduced the idea that learning is not merely something that occurs for the individual, but also for the community as it enhances its practice and develops new generations, and for the organization, which, through the interrelations of CoPs, can become more effective by, essentially, knowing what it knows.

Orr

Julian Orr, in his mid-1980s dissertation research, published in 1996 as *Talking About Machines*, studied a different type of group. We'll call it a CoP here but, in the days before the phrase "community of practice" was coined, Orr used the term "community of work." Orr's group consisted of co-workers—copier repair technicians working for IBM—who gathered at lunch and after hours to discuss problems they encountered in enacting their work. Orr watched as the technicians, in the face of inadequate repair manuals and training, frequently gathered in an unstructured, unsupervised space to discuss particular repair problems and solutions. Often the technicians, even as they successfully repaired machines, operated at philosophical odds with management. While management wanted the repair technicians to closely follow manuals and troubleshooting documentation—even if it meant machines were not fixed—the technicians often circumvented the manuals and established protocols to achieve repair. Their goal was not "to learn" but to fix a machine in the face of constraints and bad information. And in talking together to achieve this, they did learn. Orr's work shed light on several ideas perhaps not explicit in earlier literature: One, that independent of oversight, workers seek to do good work and sometimes must break rules to accomplish it. Two, the perfect worlds of the engineering unit and shop floors where manuals and new machines are created often have little relationship to the reality of fixing a machine that is used for years by people who didn't build it. And three, sometimes management—no matter how unwittingly—interferes with performance and productivity.

Bozarth

My own dissertation research focused on still another type of CoP. The pseudonymous NC TRAIN group is comprised of workplace training practitioners, all employed by North Carolina government agencies, who joined together in the early 1980s with the mission "to stamp out bad training." Since that time the group has met quarterly to demonstrate training games and activities, to share tips and frustrations, and to try out and gain feedback on new training designs. There is an annual member-presented conference, and the group provides a formal competency-based train-the-trainer course for novices. Membership is fluid, with people entering and leaving the group as job roles and life situations change; at any one time the mailing list typically includes 150 names, with perhaps forty people showing up at any particular meeting. Members report that, outside of the formal, scheduled events, they have developed relationships with others—in a sense, have developed their own training-related PLNs from within the community. This group, like Orr's, exists without formal oversight. There is no board, charter, or any formal rules (as one member said, "That would make it something else"), and the group operates independent of the auspices or supervision of any employer or agency.

Unlike the other CoPs described here, the TRAIN group exists explicitly to learn in a social way. As with Wenger's group, newcomers receive support as they move toward expertise; as with both Orr's and Wenger's groups, they learn not just to practice but *to talk about* practice. One TRAIN member understood the nuances of social learning and its role in supporting what we might call "transfer" or tacit (rather than explicit) learning: "You need to actually practice, to get into a classroom and do some training. But you also learn a lot about training by just hanging out with good trainers. You watch them, you talk to them, you pick up a lot even though you may not realize it at the time." As with Orr's group, members of NC TRAIN felt the CoP helped to overcome a management-generated limitation. Many members felt that management didn't really understand training, as opposed to what might be called "presenting," and did not care about trainer performance as long as content was delivered. Several members (and I felt this way myself in one training job I held) said they were performing at a much higher level than management expected and could succeed in their workplaces with much less effort. In interviews, several TRAIN members said they valued the CoP for giving them a place to perform with others who recognized and valued exemplary performance.

CoPs: The Next Generation?

Still another type of CoP has arisen, thanks to the advent of social media. The InSync Training, LLC Facebook group, described on page 75 as Case: Facebook as a Community for InSync Training, LLC, Course Graduates, is comprised of people who have completed InSync's certificate courses for synchronous training facilitation and design. They come from all over the world, mostly North America and the UK, and live in many time zones. As classes are small—usually fewer than fifteen people—most people joining the community may know only a few others, and even then only from online interactions during the courses. The community was formed in response to requests from graduates for "a place" they could connect with others engaged in designing and facilitating learning in the synchronous training environment, to stay in touch with friends they made in the courses, and to share tips and ideas as their practice evolved. As InSync had all the contact information on their own graduates, it was a simple enough matter to set up a Facebook group and invite everyone to join. The community manager started discussions by setting up several topics based on content addressed in the courses: use of tools available in the virtual classroom (whiteboard, chat, etc.), ideas for openers and energizers, and tips for making the synchronous learning environment more engaging and interactive. Group members quickly responded to those, then began adding their own new discussion topics, sharing articles and resources, and inviting one another to sit in on their own programs. The community manager has very little to do besides load fresh content, and every couple of weeks she sends the group an announcement—mostly for the benefit of those who have not visited in a few days—apprising members of news and new discussion topics.

Sometimes communities of practice develop deliberately, as with the NC TRAIN Group. Sometimes, as with the Orr group, the community emerges among people engaged in a joint practice. And sometimes, as with the InSync example, the CoP comes into being when the technology exists to support it. It's important to note that, with the exception of Wenger's group of claims processors employed and overseen by a single employer, the other CoPs exist without much (or in the case of TRAIN, any) oversight and supervision of the organization. In fact, the copier technicians who comprised the community in Orr's study succeeded *in spite of* management's expectations. InSync's Facebook group has minimal management in place, with the community manager responsible primarily for ensuring that fresh content is made available consistently so that members have a reason to keep visiting the group page.

The idea of a community of practice seems to be attractive to management—the phrase itself is appealing—but it is the nature of management to want to, well, manage. My dissertation research referenced the tendency among managers to want to control communities of practice, as to outsiders CoPs can seem too chaotic and unstructured. Alas, research shows that imposing control on such a community will invariably change it to something else, and as often as not will cause it to fall apart altogether. Likewise, mandating participation is just another means of control, one that is rarely successful. Several studies, most notably work from Katja Pastoors (2007), showed that forced participation is, as often as not, perceived by the individual as just more work. Their experience of the CoP in that case will not be successful—and active CoP members are likely to view them as an unwelcome intrusion.

The short answer on how organizations and the training department can support a community of practice? Give it a space to exist, provide support if it's needed, and leave it alone.

Case: Online Community Managed by Employees of Government Agency

Here's an example of another type of community, perhaps best viewed as a community of *practitioners* rather than a community of practice. A North Carolina (USA) agency workforce—comprised primarily of prison guards located across North Carolina's 550-mile span and one hundred counties— created and manages a Facebook group with the stated purpose: "This is a way to keep us as a family and not separated by the walls and fences that we work in." To this end, members do sometimes actively engage in explicitly learning from one another:

> Next month our facility will be double-bunked. I know some institutions already have this. How does it work for you guys? Will there be more fights? What have you done to manage this situation?

But the group also functions in other ways to develop and support the community, to minimize the walls and fences that concern them. It serves as a way to disseminate information or verify rumors, another form of learning:

> Has anyone heard of a new facility being built near the mountains? I heard there's going to be a 1,000-bed close custody facility.

It provides a platform for members to talk together about the sudden death of a young colleague:

> She was a lovely young woman and I'm shocked and saddened by what happened.

Given that the work of the prison guard is hard, dangerous, stressful, and often thankless, they use the group as a place to affirm what they do (and offer things that probably surprise management):

> I can actually say I love my job. I'm a career person. I have made sergeant and I'm now in the process of applying for lieutenant. Been here since 12/95 and am here to stay. I am stress-free—as far as my job is concerned, anyway.

They also use the group to manage one another:

> I want to know something. During these times of economic
> difficulties, why do people insist on not showing up for work or
> repeatedly calling out? I am tired of feeling my co-workers don't
> have my back.

Via community involvement, members support one another, minimizing
both geographical distance and the distances created by working different
shifts or work areas. They are able to overcome walls and fences. The
camaraderie and support are evident—and the learning is built in.

And Now, 268 Words About Knowledge Management

Among the terms tossed about in modern business language,
"knowledge management" is one of the most nebulous and
misunderstood. Like "community of practice," the term "knowledge
management" is appealing to leaders but subject to misunderstanding
and poor execution. As put so well by John Tropea in his blog post
http://libraryclips.blogsome.com/2005/02/07/hello_world/, the biggest
problem with "knowledge management" is that it is understood,
incorrectly, to be "information management." Asking people what they
know and putting that into a database is just managing information. Jay
Cross has written extensively on this, noting that, even if we could figure
out how to input everything everyone knows into a database, "Most of
the knowledge workers seek is tacit and beyond the reach of data-based
systems."

It is important, then, to help people find a way to connect, engage,
and learn, via PLNS or CoPs or mentoring or apprenticeships or any
other means an organization is willing to employ. But the notion of
having some senior manager decide who knows something we need to
"capture" before they retire or resign, then embarking on something
akin to a fishing expedition is just not realistic. Some organizations
have spent years trying to "harness" tacit knowledge, most without
success.

In the context of real need, few people will withhold their knowledge. A genuine request for help is not often refused unless there is literally no time or a previous history of distrust. On the other hand, ask people to codify all that they know in advance of a contextual enquiry and it will be refused (in practice it's impossible anyway). Linking and connecting people is more important than storing their artifacts.

Dave Snowden, www.cognitive-edge.com/blogs/dave/2009/03/ballerinas_and_ aircraft_carrie.php. Used with his permission.

Social Learning: How to *Do Things* Versus How to *Get Things Done*

At the beginning of this book we looked at the model of workplace training (as a series of formal events) versus where learning really happens (in between those formal events), and so far have discussed what trainers can do to get into those in-between spaces. What happens in formal training might be best described as how to *do things*: process forms, complete a performance appraisal, conduct a job interview, assemble a widget, write a policy, replace a fan belt, or create a PowerPoint show.

What happens in the spaces between formal events? Often not only how to do things, but how to *get things done*:

- Finding out who in the cashier's office will cut a check outside the usual cycle dates

- Picking up useful work-arounds

- Getting a sense of which policies are really enforced to the letter, which can be gone around, and which can be disregarded altogether

- Getting a sense of who knows what in the organization (which may have nothing to do with an organizational chart), who can be depended on for correct answers, and who keeps promises

- Knowing how and when to improvise

There are other things one learns by living in the work culture, things that cannot be explicitly taught, such as intuition about customer needs, market changes, and shifts in organizational technology use, and sensing what one's boss *really* wants, as opposed to what is written in job descriptions and performance evaluation plans.

Workers' pressing needs to get things done presents enormous opportunities for trainers trying to get "in the spaces." By helping to figure out ways we can help learners connect with one another, and being partners in the conversations they have there, we can support them in finding better ways of getting things done.

Supporting Social Learning

Mark Berthelemy: Start with the Person

Most social software projects start with the aim of encouraging creativity, knowledge sharing, and collaboration. This is to be achieved by providing tools that allow people to make connections with each other, collaborate on work, and share what they know.

Often, very little thought is given to how those tools will actually be used, how the individuals concerned will learn how to use them, what motivation they will have to use them, and how that motivation will be sustained.

For successful social learning projects, we must remember that we're dealing with people, with needs, desires, other priorities, and varying levels of confidence.

Social learning starts with the individual. It's the individual who chooses to contribute. It's the individual who learns. It's the individual who makes connections to other individuals. Only then, through those connections, can the group, the organization, learn and change.

(Continued)

> So, rather than immediately putting people into a collaborative environ-
> ment, expecting them to create knowledge together, my recommendation
> would always be to take it steady and start with demonstrating the useful-
> ness of social learning to the individual. Creating a space for networking
> is fine, but how will you stimulate people to actually **do** that networking?
> Of course, if you're working with a group that is already motivated to
> generate knowledge collaboratively, then you can bypass a lot of this.
>
> http://www.learningconversations.co.uk/main/index.php/2009/11/19/getting-
> started-with-social-software-for-learning?blog=5. Used with permission of Mark
> Berthelemy.

What's the Future?

Increasingly, in the face of so many new tools and worker-driven
initiatives toward professional development, we are facing a world in
which training as we know it will just no longer remain viable. The idea
of "learning" occurring only within the confines of four walls and a
facilitator, or with a learner being tracked as he completes an online
tutorial, is simply being outpaced by technologies that can enable so
much more. This needn't be a threat to trainers, who in the new
environment (as I've noted several times in this book) will be able to
repurpose many skills they already possess. In many instances they may
just be employing existing skills while using new tools.

There's one more area that may need development, and it involves the
space where the trainer "lives." Have you ever heard a learner say in
class, "That's not how we do it back on the job"? Or worse, have you
ever have a new hire, upon freshly retuning to work after training, report
that co-workers told him to disregard what he or she heard in training?
If learning professionals are to support knowledge management in
helping learners understand how to get things done, then we will need
to learn ourselves how things get done. If you're in a large organization
you may never learn the subtleties of all the processes and relationships,
but you can learn more about the learners' work contexts and their
barriers to more effective performance.

New View of Training

At the beginning of this book we looked at the traditional model of workplace training versus where learning really happens, and so far have discussed what trainers can do to get into those formal spaces. Here, again, are the images courtesy Bob Mosher, in Figures 7.1 and 7.2.

Figure 7.1. Traditional Model of Workplace Training

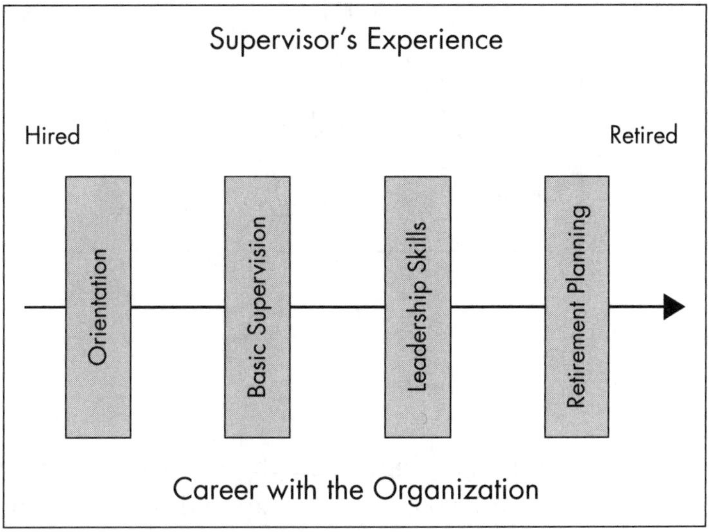

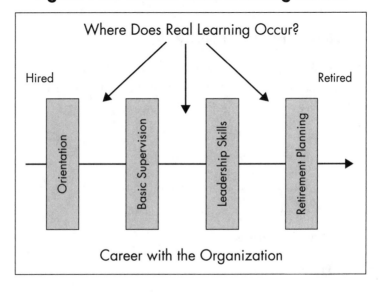

Figure 7.2. Where Real Learning Occurs

Figure 7.3. New Model of Workplace Training

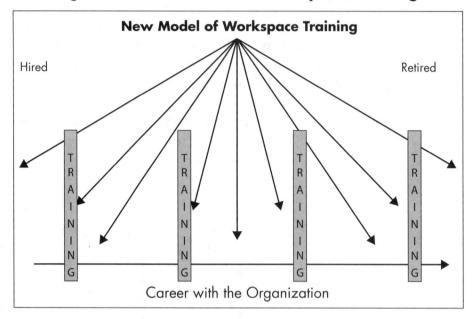

In Figure 7.3 is what training might look like in a few years, with formal events shorter and spaced farther apart, but with trainers much more heavily engaged with workers between the formal events of the former model.

Getting Started with Social Learning

When you're ready to get started with social learning, try beginning with the checklist below from Dave Wilkins and Kevin D. Jones. Who owns what? How will you get from Point A to Point B? How will you mitigate risk?

Social Learning Strategies Checklist

❑ What kinds of social media are already being used in the organization?

❑ For what purpose?

❑ Who owns them?

❑ What kinds of learning communities do you want to help along through hands-on nurturing?

❑ What kinds of learning communities do you want to more proactively manage and plan?

❑ What are the problems you are trying to solve?

❑ Who is your target member for your community?

❑ What are the problems your community members are trying to solve?

❑ If the problems are solved, what does success look like?

❑ If the problems are solved, what is the impact of success?

❑ What is your social learning policy?

❑ What is your plan when these policies are breached?

❑ What is in your "Miss Manners" guide to social learning?

❑ Who is on your social learning governance board: IT, Legal, CLO etc.?

❑ How will social learning activities factor into key performance indicators and performance reviews?

❑ What does IT own? Some suggestions: security issues, archiving, technical issues, deployment, options, aggregation, report consolidation, integration fulfillment, report fulfillment.

❑ What does Learning own? Some suggestions: strategy, cultural readiness, "tools" training, moderation, member management, community management, programming, integration requirements, reporting fulfillment with built-in reporting tools.

❑ What does Legal and Compliance own? Some suggestions: archival strategy, social media storage requirements, approval strategies for sensitive content (which might be all content), member management and "flagging" policies, reporting requirements for all of the above.

❑ Who will support your organization's use of social media? Technical support? IT? Learning?

❑ What is your start point in terms of participants and technologies?

❑ What is the long-term rollout plan? What social media tools will be turned on when? When you do turn on new functionality, what is the trigger: time, membership, activity?

❑ Will you organize content topically, hierarchically by division, unit etc., or by functional area?

❑ What is your launch strategy to drive participation? (More below.)

❑ What is your moderation strategy?

❑ What is your reporting strategy?

❑ Who will own your programming schedule?

❑ How will you identify champions and key influencers prior to roll out on an ongoing basis?

❑ Who will be responsible for defining content categories and the overall ontology of your social learning content?

❑ What is end of life or end game for your learning community? Does the community evolve into something else? Is it archived? Is there a planned obsolescence because it's a one-off in response to external factors what will change?

Social Learning Strategies checklist from Dave Wilkins and Kevin D. Jones; provided under the Creative Commons Share Alike license.

Summary

The trainer actively participating in social networking and social learning activities will likely prove him- or herself a critical player in supporting workplace learning, learners, and the goals of the organization. As with the other tools and approaches we've seen, it's important to keep the big picture in mind: What are you trying to accomplish, and what will help you get there? In the words of Karl Kaopp: "People don't share business insights, innovations, and concepts just because technology is available; they share because they feel everyone is working toward a common goal" (Karl Kapp, http://karlkapp.blogspot.com).

Be the Change

In this book I have outlined technologies and activities to be used specifically in training within the purview of the individual trainer or the training department. But social media tools in business aren't really maximized by containing them in that way. Social media allow for work units, professions, colleagues, and whole organizations to better connect, share, and learn, all while spanning space and time. Helping organizations view knowledge as belonging to the collective good, rather than as proprietary pieces of data, and encouraging movement toward a culture of sharing will benefit you, training, and the organization.

Selling the Change

Not all senior leaders are ready to embrace this technology and may need some convincing. You can be an informed advocate. Here are some tips:

- Tie the change to a business need, not a "cool" technology play. The fact that a tool has x million users or "everyone is using it" won't matter to management. How will it solve a real problem?

- Solve a real problem.

- How much time do workers spend looking for information? Would a wiki help?

- What problems are caused by the disconnected communications among engineers in several national offices? Could Twitter help?

- How much time and trouble does it take to offer formal updates about research and competitor information? Would a blog solve that problem?

- Show how competitors are using tools effectively.

- Approach the issue from the point of view of individual parts of the organization.

  - What could the use of social media do to improve customer relations? How could it help HR in recruiting?

  - What are ways to support R&D's need to stay current?

- Identify different strategies for different groups. (This is known as "eating the elephant one bite at a time.")

- Remind management that employees are talking about the company. Would they prefer that be inside or outside of company walls?

- Watch your terminology. Be careful of words like "socializing" and "media" and talk instead about "knowledge management," "knowledge networks," "collaboration technology," and "problem resolution."

- Build partnerships with your organization's early adopters, innovators, and other technology lovers. They will likely be willing to try out and help you field test ideas, giving you a real example and making you more fluent both with the products and in talking about and demonstrating them to higher-ups. You'll also have allies if (or, face it, when) the naysayers grumble.

- If management is worried about security issues, suggest alternatives such as internally hosted blogs, wikis, or Yammer (a product similar to Twitter designed for corporate use).

- If management is worried about people "wasting time" on Facebook, or Twitter, or anywhere else, remind them that these are problems on the individual-performer level. If an employee is abusing time on the telephone, we don't take out all the telephones.

- Be realistic. What is the nature of your company's culture? Would a stranger walking through the building think that "sharing" is a defining element? Is there a good deal of common space and chatter? Or are there lots of closed doors and formal, structured meetings? If so the time may not be right to launch a social media initiative. But the time is always right to start introducing the idea of social media.

- Stop talking. Demonstrate a successful Facebook learning page. Invite management into a Twitter conversation about best books *for leaders*. Run a small pilot project with a group creating a "best practices for phlebotomists" wiki. Just telling people how Twitter "works" is not going to work.

- Lead a "safe web" program to heighten awareness of appropriate participation on social media sites, how to manage privacy settings on sites like Facebook, how to protect photos on Flickr, etc.

Being the Change

It is easy to fall into the "my organization won't let me" or "our culture isn't like that" trap. Sometimes it's true, sometimes it's convenient, often it is a matter of someone not asking or someone not understanding what's being asked. Become educated and familiar with the tools. Be willing to try something out on your own time or your own computer. Get a small group of learners to try something with you. You need to be the change. Here are closing words from Steve Radick:

"Don't tell me it's too hard or that your boss doesn't know YouTube from an iPod. Those are excuses, not reasons. If YouTube is blocked where you work, get it unblocked. Write a white paper justifying why it shouldn't be blocked. Meet with your boss about it. Meet with your boss's boss about it. Start a blog where you talk about it. Volunteer to give a brown-bag presentation to your office. Just DO something! Take the initiative and work on changing how your organization works—don't just sit there sulking, saying, "I wish we could do social media here, but we can't even get on Facebook so there's no use." Bringing social media to your organization isn't something that happens from 9 to 5. It happens from 5 to 9, after everyone else has gone home.

"I know it's not easy. In fact, it's going to be REALLY hard. Hard, but definitely not impossible. You're going to face a lot of opposition. You're going to encounter a lot of nay-sayers. . . . More than likely though, you'll become recognized. You'll be noticeable. You'll be in demand. Most importantly, you'll make a difference."

Excerpted from http://steveradick.com/2008/12/14/stop-the-posturing-about-government-20-and-do-it-already/. Used with permission of Steve Radick.

APPENDIX

Table A.1 is a quick overview of the primary tools covered in this book. Early readers asked for something like a comparison chart, and I offer it with some hesitation. I have tried to show that the tools are largely flexible. The creative trainer can find ways to bend and flex them to meet myriad needs. For instance, it's true that wikis are good for supporting collaborative discussion, but the other tools can be used for discussion as well. To say that Twitter is good for getting quick, concise responses does not mean that's all you can use it for, nor does it mean that you can't receive the same responses with another tool. In choosing tools, consider which will best support your overall strategy and the performance objectives for your learners, as well as which are most easily accessible and appealing to your learners within your particular work culture.

Table A.1. Product Comparison Chart

	In a Nutshell	Bigger Picture	How to View It
Twitter	Microblogging tool that allows users to publish chronologically ordered "tweets" of 140 characters or fewer.	Tweets feed into a timeline that you and others can view. Good for rapid conversation, quick answers, live chats.	Those who read tweets are meant to drink from the stream; while as a trainer you can manage discussion and assignments to some extent, Twitter is not in general a vehicle for linear, structured conversation.
Facebook	Single-login site that aggregates many forms of social media, such as messages, photos, videos, events, discussions, and hobbies.	A great deal of functionality available to users, who can post status updates, links, photos, and multimedia such as videos; users can join groups.	One-stop community portal with functionality for groups, discussions, event planning, links, photos, videos, and online games and quizzes. Private messaging and live chat available. Can be used to host a course.
Blog	Online space for posting chronologically ordered comments or ideas that can include text, photo, video, audio, and links to other sites, blogs, or documents. Readers can respond to posted content.	Easy, one-stop, do-it-yourself web-page creation tool. Allows for adding images and multimedia; simple post-and-respond interaction.	Space for reflection, post-and-response conversation, and knowledge sharing. Clean, simple space for arranging assignments, discussion questions, and links to course material. Can be used to host course.

| **Wiki** | Interactive web page on which everyone with access can change the content. | Easy-to-use, editable online space for collaborative work, sharing knowledge, and building databases or libraries of information. | Most useful for collaboration, editorship, and data compilation. Examples in training: learner-built development of permanent, takeaway record of a particular course session; record of course over various iterations or offerings across time; compilation of FAQs or good practices for those coming into the role that the training targets; or single project aimed at improving overall company or work-unit operations. |

REFERENCES AND SUGGESTED READING

References

Bandura, A. (1977). *Social learning theory.* New York: General Learning Press.

Bozarth, J. (2008). The usefulness of Wenger's framework in understanding a community of practice. Unpublished doctoral dissertation available at www.lib.ncsu.edu/theses/available/etd-11042008-150721/unrestricted/etd.pdf (or Google "Jane Bozarth dissertation").

Cross, J. (2010). *Working smarter: Informal learning in the cloud.* Berkeley, CA: Lulu.

Deloitte. (2009). *State of the media democracy* (4th ed.). Chicago: Author.

Dobbs, K. (2000, January). Simple moments of learning. *Training, 135,* 52–57.

Kouzes J., Posner, B., & Bozarth, J. (2010). *The challenge continues.* San Francisco: Pfeiffer.

Kupritz, V.W. (2002). The relative impact of workplace design on training transfer. *Human Resource Development Quarterly, 13*(4), 427–447.

Orr, J. (1996). *Talking about machines: An ethnography of a modern job.* New York: Cornell University Press.

Pastoors, K. (2007).Consultants: Love-hate relationships with communities of practice *The Learning Organization: The International Journal of Knowledge and Organizational Learning Management*, 14(1), 21–33.

Quinn, C. (2009, February 23). Networking: Bridging formal and informal learning. *Learning Solutions magazine*. www .learningsolutionsmag.com.

Shank, P. (2007). *The online learning idea book*. San Francisco: Pfeiffer.

Vygotsky, L.S. (1962). *Thought and language*. Cambridge, MA: MIT Press.

Vygotsky, L.S., & Cole, M. (1978). *Mind in society: The development of higher psychological processes*. Cambridge, MA: Harvard University Press.

Wenger, E. (1999). *Communities of practice: learning, meaning, and identity*. New York: Cambridge University Press.

Suggested Reading

Here are a few suggested resources for readers; some focused on training and trainers, some dealing with social media and social learning, and some dealing with change management. Some are also included above in the References for this book.

Barbazette, J. (2004). *Instant case studies: How to design, adapt, and use case studies in training*. San Francisco: Pfeiffer.

Bingham, T., & Conner, M. (2010). *The new social learning: A guide to transforming organizations through social media*. New York and San Francisco: ASTD and Berrett-Koehler.

Block, P. (2003). *The answer to how is yes: Acting on what matters*. San Francisco: Berrett-Koehler.

Bozarth, J. (2008). The usefulness of Wenger's framework in understanding a community of practice. Unpublished doctoral dissertation available at www.lib.ncsu.edu/theses/available/etd-11042008-150721/unrestricted/etd.pdf (or Google "Jane Bozarth dissertation").

Cross, J. (2010). *Working smarter: Informal learning in the cloud*. Berkeley, CA: Lulu.

Gawande, A. (2009). *The checklist manifesto: How to get things right.* New York: Metropolitan Books.

Honold, L. (2000). *Developing learners who love to learn.* Palo Alto, CA: Davies-Black. (N.B.: Do not dismiss this one because of the publication date. It is full of realistic, clear, examples for ways the trainers can support development of a learning culture.)

Kapp, K. (2007). *Gadgets, games and gizmos for learning.* San Francisco: Pfeiffer.

Li, C., & Bernoff, J. (2008). *Groundswell: Winning in a world transformed by social technologies.* Cambridge, MA: Harvard University Press.

Orr, J. (1996). *Talking about machines: An ethnography of a modern job.* New York: Cornell University Press.

Rogers, E. (2003). *Diffusion of innovations.* New York: The Free Press.

Schank, R. (2005). *Lessons in learning, e-learning, and training.* San Francisco: Pfeiffer.

Note: The most current thinking on social media tools and applications will be found online. An excellent online place to start is Jane Hart's's Centre for Learning and Performance Technologies website at www .c4lpt.co.uk, an exhaustive, constantly updated compendium of tools, products, experts, and information on all things e-learning and many things social and informal learning. As products and websites are so prone to launching and changing, with updates appearing all the time, readers are also encouraged to Google for recent news in "social media"; to follow Twitterers who participate in #lrnchat or come up in searches for "e-learning," "social learning," and "social media," and to look for Facebook groups and fan pages and LinkedIn discussions referencing similar terms.

ABOUT THE AUTHOR

Jane Bozarth is an internationally known trainer, speaker, and author. A training practitioner since 1989, Jane is a graduate of the University of North Carolina at Chapel Hill, has an M.Ed. in training and development/technology in training from North Carolina State University, and completed her doctorate in training and development in 2008. She is the author of Pfeiffer's *e-Learning Solutions on a Shoestring; Better Than Bullet Points: Creating Engaging e-Learning with PowerPoint; From Analysis to Evaluation,* and, with Jim Kouzes and Barry Posner, *The Challenge Continues.* In addition to her work as e-learning coordinator for the state of North Carolina, Jane has a longstanding collaborative relationship with InSync Training, LLC, and serves as their social media strategist.

Jane is the recipient of a Live and Online Award, a *Training* magazine Editor's Pick Award, and a North Carolina State University Distinguished Alumni Award for Outstanding Contributions to Practice.

Jane and her husband, Kent Underwood, live in Durham, North Carolina. She can be contacted via her website www.bozarthzone.com, via Facebook at Jane Bozarth Bozarthzone, and via Twitter at @janebozarth.